Praise for Robert M. Meisner and *Condo Living*

"Everything you need to know about condo living. Meisner tells you what they are—what your rights are or aren't—what you need to look out for. If you live in or are thinking of buying a condominium, you need this book. Read it before you sign on the dotted line."

GLENN HAEGE
AMERICA'S MASTER HANDYMAN

"As a lawyer and condominium board member, this unique treatise of knowledge and wisdom should be a must-read for any professional who directly or indirectly is involved in counseling or managing condominiums. No one should be without this valuable, enjoyable and sometimes humorous resource."

HERBERT KAY, ESQ.
PRESIDENT, UNITED CONDOMINIUM OWNERS OF MICHIGAN

"As a developer for more than 35 years, I can attest that Bob Meisner's expose' on condominiums is a must-read for anyone attempting to develop and/or operate a condominium or community association. *Condo Living*'s insight into condo development and condo law is unsurpassed and invaluable to anyone who wants to learn about successful condominium development from the ground up."

BERNIE GLIEBERMAN
CEO, CROSSWINDS COMMUNITIES

"As an officer and member of a condo association board for more than 15 years, I can tell you that *Condo Living* is a descriptive triumph for anyone serving on a board of directors and/or officer of a condominium association. (Meisner's) knowledge and ability to articulate the problems attendant with condominiums and how to avoid them have been a help in my duties as a fiduciary to my condominium association."

DR. FRED BERNSTEIN
DIRECTOR/BOARD MEMBER, KEATING NEW TOWN ASSOCIATION

More Praise for Robert M. Meisner and *Condo Living*

"I wish we had known about this book before my wife and I purchased our condominium unit. Fortunately, we read it before selling our condo. The information clearly defines the selling and legal requirements, describes some major potential problems that can occur, and how to avoid them. It's a great resource filled with important tips."

CLARENCE MORGAN
FORMER PRESIDENT, CONDOMINIUM BOARD OF DIRECTORS

"If you want to know what it is really like to live in a condominium and you are thinking about purchasing one as a primary residence or a second home or recreational abode, Bob Meisner's book is an indispensable tool to gain the knowledge you must have before entering into a purchase agreement. Bob's insightful and clear explanation of the realities and vagaries of condominium living has not, in my opinion, been matched to date by any written materials on the subject."

EILEEN GULLICK
RETIRED EDUCATOR

CONDO LIVING

A SURVIVAL GUIDE
to Buying, Owning and
Selling a Condominium

BY ROBERT M. MEISNER, ESQ.
Illustrations by Marty Harris

Momentum Books, L.L.C.
Troy, Michigan

Published by Momentum Books, L.L.C., a subsidiary of Hour Media, L.L.C.

2145 Crooks Road, Suite 208
Troy, MI 48084
www.momentumbooks.com

Printed and bound in the U.S.A.

ISBN-13: 978-1-879094-74-1
ISBN-10: 1-879094-74-6
LCCN: 2005934481

This book is dedicated to my two sons:
Derek, the lawyer, and Randy, the doctor.

TABLE OF CONTENTS

PREFACE

The names and events depicted in this book are fictional and, although based upon real-life experiences of the author, are not intended to describe any actual person, entity or event. Any similarity to any person, living or dead, or to any entity or event, is purely coincidental!

A NOTE TO THE READER:

Both men and women buy condos, but to ease the reader's burden, I will use "he" to stand for both except for occasional references to "he or she" in order to remind us that either gender could be involved.

WHAT'S IN A NAME?

Have you noticed that condominium developers often come up with the most idyllic names for condominium projects? Developers try to paint a rosy picture of condominium living, and one of the best marketing ideas is a name that conveys that attitude. Utopian sounding names, such as "Green Farms," "Pleasant Acres," "The Woods," "Windmill Pointe," "Oakwood Park," "Pebblecreek," "Highland Lakes" and "Streamwood" are common. So, too, the developer may invoke the names of places in old England, or other parts of Europe, to convey its marketing message. Names like "Coventry," "Stonehenge," "Londonderry Downs," "English Colony," "Colonial Village," "Brittany" and "Le Chateau" convey an image of solitude, peacefulness, tranquility and castle-like habitability.

We should stress truth in condominium labeling, as we already have truth in lending, truth in renting and truth in packaging. Condominiums should be no different. In fact, I'd love to live in a condo that was honest enough to call itself "The Palaces of Saddam!"

Wouldn't it be more truthful if the condo developer, who is converting a run-down apartment complex into a condominium and selling the units "as is" and "without warranties," were to market his project as "The Leaning Tower," instead of "Fox and Hounds?" A condominium named "Lake in the Woods," known by the developer to have a history of erosion and pollution problems, probably would be more accurately named "Waste Disposal Gardens."

Perhaps developers ought to borrow names from great battles, such as "Waterloo," "The Bulge" or "The Alamo," to describe the confrontations that, no doubt, will occur among some residents of a condo. The Nazi-like attitude conveyed by some directors would lend itself to a project known as "Gestapo Gardens." And wouldn't it be more realistic if a condo populated with chronic malcontents, distraught with the actions of the directors, no matter what they do, were referred to as "Nuthouse Villas" or "Freud Landings?"

Sure, it would hurt the developer's marketing program, but it might also convey a more realistic message to the prospective condominium purchaser. In fact, such changes would ultimately avoid litigation because purchasers would know exactly what they are getting into when they buy!

THE REALITY OF CONDO LIVING AND GOVERNANCE

Many readers will think I had perpetual heartburn and indigestion when I wrote this book. I did not.

My central theme is that condominium living is not for everyone. Condominium living is replete with pitfalls, trials and tribulations. Anyone who is interested in buying a condominium, regardless of his socio-economic, religious, geographic or age group, should be aware of the legal and practical aspects of life in a condominium.

What should be emphasized, as well, is that one must have a particular personality and disposition to enjoy condominium living. That conclusion would apply whether the prospective purchaser is single, retired or married without children. (My focus on these groups is not intended to suggest condominiums should not be occupied, or cannot be enjoyed, by families with children. That is not, however, one of the most common types of condominium purchaser, since condominiums typically are either apartments or townhouses located in a confined setting that is not conducive to the rearing of large families, which typically require open spaces to play and run.)

"IT TAKES ALL KINDS"

Let's look for a moment at the three types of people most likely to consider buying a condo, and consider whether the condominium lifestyle is for them: singles, retirees and married without children.

The first type of condo purchaser I will discuss is the single.

Mistakenly, and without the "advice of counsel," I bought a condominium during my divorce. Perhaps the trauma of the divorce temporarily asphyxiated my brain cells. Whatever the reason, I thought I could get along in a condominium project which had been managed for 15 years by residents who:

- Rarely sought legal advice (and when they did, called on residents of the condominium to give them "free" advice);

- Built up no reserve fund because a real estate agent thought it would increase the monthly assessment to the extent that the condominium would become unmarketable; and,

- Were more concerned about the landscaping program than repairing cracks in the walls of units.

Generally, however, single people find condominiums attractive because they will not have to worry about the exterior maintenance and will enjoy social and recreational amenities that may not be available to them in a single-family dwelling. Unlike a rental apartment, they expect their investment will build equity, which may be true in the right circumstances.

My experience as a single person living in a condominium is that these expectations may be realized if the other problems common to condominium living can be avoided. If you don't care how the association really works, so long as your grass is cut and the roof is fixed, then living in a condo may be the answer. Unfortunately, "carefree maintenance" is beneficial to a single person only if the association discharges its legal and fiduciary responsibilities for maintenance.

Moreover, the single person who has wild parties in his condominium unit will soon find he is an unpopular resident and the target of letters or litigation, or both, brought by his neighbors or the condominium association. Finally, if the single person has a mind of his own and is concerned about the possibility of an abusive board of directors, he may smartly retreat to a single-family detached home (not a site condominium) and stay out of the bureaucratic morass that frequently exists in condominium communities!

If the condominium project is composed primarily of retirees, the tolerance of the board of directors toward youthful singles may be a problem. I have experienced instances where singles have bought units in a retirement community only to be subjected to the consternation of neighbors and, eventually, the board of directors, over the nighttime presence of male or female guests.

If you are a single person, are considering a condominium and have evaluated all of the other aspects of condominium living, make sure that you won't be a social outcast. In particular, make sure your lifestyle will mesh with the lifestyle of most other association members. In my experience, being single and living in a condo was not a problem from the standpoint of disturbances by my neighbors. However, I lived in a semi-detached townhouse separated from the adjoining townhouses by a common wall, a physical configuration that reduced the proximity of residents. By contrast, an apartment-style condominium, where people may live both above and below, may lead to noise problems ranging from dropped shoes to late night parties.

At the risk of sounding chauvinistic, condominium living may be particularly good for a single woman who lacks the time, skills or desire to maintain a single-family home on her own. The condominium may provide her with enhanced security and camaraderie, usually without the responsibility to cut the grass and perform exterior maintenance and repairs.

Retirees, the second group of condo purchasers, may find condominium living advantageous because they may, as they prefer, participate in, or dissociate themselves from, the affairs of the association community. Having been involved in such activities throughout their lives, they may now be looking for a time to rest. The risk, if these persons do not participate, is that they are deferring to persons whose life experiences and skills may not equip them to perform these responsibilities.

On the other hand, if the retiree is looking for a situation where the monthly assessments will not go up and there is no potential for controversy, condominium living may not be the answer. Eventually, the common elements will need to be repaired or replaced, and the monthly assessments may need to be increased, sometimes significantly, to meet these needs. The condominium that is composed primarily of retired people on fixed incomes may not be the place for a young married couple or a single person to invest, because the board, which presumably will be composed of retirees, may not be disposed to spend the money necessary to deal with the problems and long-term concerns of the condominium. In this book, I hope to make the reader aware of the practices of developers and condominium association boards which may lead to unexpected problems that produce conflict between the interests of these groups.

Things that seem simple and harmless on the surface may be a problem as well. For instance, if the retiree wants to plant flowers, he'd better make certain that the association doesn't have an absolute prohibition on the planting of flowers!

In general, condominiums that are dominated by persons of a single marital status, age group or socio-economic group are not good, since the decisions of that association will tend to be parochial and reflective of the particular needs of that group.

For example, a condominium composed exclusively of retired corporate executives will not necessarily be well managed or an enjoyable place to live. The "country club" mentality of the directors may not lend itself well to the operation of the association. Moreover, although the modern corporate executive may promote an atmosphere in which ideas are welcomed, corporate executives who encourage dissenting views remain rare.

A more diverse composition of members—some retirees, some newly-married, some single, some affluent and some of more limited means—creates a mix that is beneficial to the condominium's success. In short, a diversity of personalities is, in my experience, better for the success of the association.

An exception may be senior citizen housing, including condominium housing for retired persons. Here, like-minded residents may share their concerns and participate in the various social and recreational activities that are available, while excluding families with children, if they qualify under the amendment to the Federal Fair Housing Act of 1989. Even here, however, unique problems may arise because of the general unwillingness of senior citizens to expend the money necessary to properly operate the affairs of the association and repair and replace the common elements.

Condominium living is not for everyone. It is not for people who do not have the economic means to properly sustain the operation of the association and to deal with its problems. Perhaps apartment living for those people is more appropriate. Senior citizens who read this book should keep this in mind in making the decisions necessary to operate the affairs of the association.

We come at last to the third common type of condo purchaser: married couples without children. Having lived in an apartment, two condominiums and several single-family suburban houses, I can unequivocally state that if you are going to raise a family, do so in a detached, single-family subdivision or site condominium rather than an apartment or attached condominium. This assumes, of course, that you have a choice. If you live in Manhattan, there is little chance of your finding an affordable, single-family detached dwelling. If you live in Great Neck, Long Island, the circumstances may be different.

In the typical "traditional," or apartment-style, condominium, any exterior modifications, including basketball hoops and roof aerials, must be approved by the condominium board of directors. More significantly, kids make noise, want to play outside, have friends over and engage in activities that other residents, particularly those who are senior citizens or who are childless, may find annoying and objectionable. (Keep in mind that most senior citizens have been through the child-rearing years and are no longer interested in dealing with its rigors, except for the occasional visit of their grandchildren on a Sunday afternoon.) Finally, a major problem in condominiums, from the standpoint of the board, is children who abuse the condominium premises.

It is no secret that many traditional condominium projects do not like children within their confines, and I frequently am requested to draft condominium document provisions barring them. Federal legislation barring discrimination on the basis of age has rendered such prohibitions unenforceable, with the exception of qualifying "senior citizen" communities (that is, age 55 and older). Consequently, it is illegal for a developer or condominium association to preclude children from living in a condominium.

Nevertheless, there often develops a sub-current of discontent when someone with children buys an attached condominium unit. Unless you are buying a unit in a condominium with numerous young marrieds with children, you are best advised to examine very carefully whether living in a condominium with children is a viable option for you, notwithstanding federal laws that purportedly protect you.

This is not to say that people with families cannot bring them up in condominiums. Again, it depends on the pertinent state and federal laws, the physical structure of the condominium unit itself, the restrictions imposed on co-owners and the attitude of the board of directors and managing agent toward family activities.

If you have a choice of housing, raise your family instead in a single-family subdivision, where the restrictions are minimal and the open spaces greater. That is not to say that homeowner associations do not have clout concerning the enforcement of deed restrictions on single-family residents within that subdivision. Still, the restrictions in a homeowner's subdivision are generally not as pervasive and encompassing as those found in a condominium, even if that condominium is a "site" condominium.

A "site" condominium is a form of condominium in which all, or a portion, of the land is subdivided and sold as individual building sites, or condominium units, on which a co-owner may construct a dwelling. To the casual observer, a site condominium unit may be indistinguishable from a subdivision lot. In the site condominium, both the interior and exterior of the dwelling, and the other improvements located on the building site, are maintained by the individual co-owner, and not the condominium association, although the condominium association usually will retain exterior aesthetic control.

In summary, condominium living can be beneficial and an enjoyable experience. A condominium unit can be financially rewarding and a good investment. Co-owners can avoid physical work, time and, in some instances, the expenses of maintaining a single-family, detached dwelling. Condominium living offers social, recreational, vocational and psychological benefits to its inhabitants. It also can provide enhanced security, reduction of fixed costs and additional amenities that would not normally be affordable to residents in other types of living environments. It can offer an opportunity to participate in a community governing structure while gaining self-fulfillment from the knowledge that one is making a contribution. It can offer residents a place to live that demands only a minimal commitment to the governing structure and to the maintenance of the condominium community. It can be all of these things, but only to the person who has the right temperament, personality and socio-economic standing for that condominium. The person who wishes the freedom to live in his dwelling and its environs as he sees fit, without interference from any quasi-municipal governing structure, is not such a person. A farm would be a better place for that person!

ABOUT THIS BOOK

It should already be apparent to the reader that, through my experiences as a condominium owner and attorney, I have established my own criteria for good condominium living. In the following pages, I will share my opinions and guidelines. This book is organized as follows: Part One discusses the factors to be considered when selecting, buying and selling a condominium. Part Two explains the management and operation of condominium associations. Finally, I have appended my maxims, which I have collected over the years in the hope of shedding some humorous light on my subject.

Sincerely,
Bob Meisner

P.S. The cartoons were added in case you start to take me too seriously.

PART I Buying and Selling a Condo

Condominium living is not for everyone. There are numerous factors to consider before taking the plunge. Here's how to select, buy and sell a condo.

CHAPTER 1

I'm Buying *What?*
Understanding Condos and Their Terms

Since condominiums are the focus of this book, it would appear necessary to fully acquaint the reader with what a condominium really is, as opposed to what you may have seen in movies or on TV, read in a newspaper ad or heard from a friend or relative who lives in one. You may even own a condominium, but not have a realistic idea of the legal and practical aspects of condominium living.

Condominium is not a new concept in housing. The word "condominium" comes from a Latin word meaning "common ownership or control." The Romans had condominiums, and during the Middle Ages, they were popular in the walled cities of Western Europe. During the first half of the 20th century, several European countries enacted statutes permitting condominiums.

Although a few condominiums existed in the United States as early as 1947, they were not authorized by any state statute prior to 1961. By now, most states have enacted some form of statute regulating the formation and operation of condominiums. Initially, many states adopted, either totally or in substantial part, the Uniform Condominium Act, a model residential condominium act. In Michigan, for example, the Horizontal Real Property Act, enacted in 1963, was modeled upon the Uniform Condominium Act. Because this law proved inadequate to meet the needs of the fast-growing condominium industry, the Michigan Condominium Act was enacted in 1978. In many states, second-generation, and even third-generation, condominium statutes have been enacted to address problems that were not envisioned or properly dealt with in the original enabling legislation.

Most condominium statutes are designed to regulate the rights and responsibilities between: 1) The purchaser of a condominium unit and the developer of the condominium project; and 2) The co-owner of a condominium unit and the association of co-owners.

The reader may ask, "How does a condominium differ from a cooperative?" A cooperative is a residential housing project that is owned by a cooperative corporation. When you buy an interest in a typical cooperative, you become the owner of shares of stock in the cooperative association that owns all of the real estate of the cooperative, including the residential units. Generally, you then enter into a proprietary lease with the cooperative association that allows you to occupy a residential unit. In short, you do not own the residential unit in which you live, but instead, you own a share of stock in the cooperative association and you rent your unit. While cooperatives have been popular in the Eastern cities and in Chicago, they have not caught on as a major form of residential development in other parts of the United States.

Before you purchase a condominium unit, it is important to understand what the purchaser of a condominium unit typically buys: namely, an undivided interest in common areas and a cubicle of space within a commonly owned project.

Ordinarily, condominium unit ownership means the exclusive individual ownership of the space inside the inner walls of an apartment or townhouse, and common ownership of the surrounding structures and underlying land. This division between exclusive and common ownership exists regardless of the form or design of the condominium project.

Although the focus of this book is the residential condominium, the reader should keep in mind that there are many other types of condominiums. Commercial condominiums are extremely popular as office space for professionals, and high-rise buildings containing a combination of commercial and residential condominiums (lofts) now dot the major cities of our hemisphere. Industrial condominiums are utilized for warehousing and factory facilities. Mobile home condominiums are catching on throughout North America. And campsite condominiums are popular in recreational areas. Time-share condominiums are widely advertised in vacation spots around the world. There are even parking lot condominiums, not only in the center of major cities but near football stadia and other sports facilities. Speaking of football stadia, Ford Field, the home of the Detroit Lions and the site of the 2006 Super Bowl, was developed as a condominium!

In the residential context, the project, as it is often called, may take the physical form of a high-rise townhouse building containing two or more areas of exclusive individual ownership. The project may instead consist of two or more individually owned single-family, detached dwellings constructed upon the commonly owned land. Or, in the site condominium context, the land and air space comprising the entire envelope of the building site, together with the physical structure, may be individually owned.

In a mobile home, campground, marina or parking site condominium, the area of exclusive ownership may be limited to a cube of air space within which a mobile home, recreational vehicle or car is parked or a boat is anchored. The elements of common ownership might then be the utility systems and the land or water improvements, such as concrete pads in the mobile home park, piers in a marina or a clubhouse in a recreational condominium.

The condominium unit, which is the portion of the condominium that the purchaser individually owns, is his or hers exclusively to decorate, maintain, live in and use. Usually, everything else in the condominium project, that is, the exterior walls, the commonly owned land, the common hallways in an apartment-style building, the recreational facilities, etc., constitute the "common elements," the commonly-owned property of everyone who owns a condominium unit in the project. So, in effect, a "condominium" is nothing more than a form of ownership in which portions of the property are owned by ALL owners of the condominium project, namely, the "co-owners," as they are referred to in the condominium documents and most enabling statutes.

Some of these "common elements," such as patios, balconies, garages and carport spaces, although owned by all co-owners, are limited and restricted in use to the co-owner of the condominium unit they serve and his family. These common elements are generally referred to as "limited common elements." Other "limited common elements," such as stairways or laundry facilities, may be limited and restricted to use by all residents who live in that building. The remainder of the common elements, such as the land itself, roads, green areas, recreational facilities and, in some instances, the outer walls, foundations, roofs and other structural elements of the building, are termed "general common elements." The general common elements are available for the use, at least theoretically, of everyone who has an ownership interest in the condominium project. Both the limited common elements and general common elements, however, remain the common property of all the co-owners in the project.

Before you purchase a condominium unit, you also should understand the roles of the various entities which, typically, are involved in its organization, ownership and operation: 1) the developer; 2) the co-owner; 3) the association of co-owners; 4) the board of directors of the association of co-owners; and 5) the managing agent.

Too often, in my experience, the purchaser or resident of a condominium lacks an accurate understanding of his or her rights and/or responsibilities because he or she does not understand the respective roles, rights and responsibilities of the persons involved in the development and operation of the condominium project.

The "developer" is the person who has organized the condominium project and is responsible under the state enabling statute for doing so. The description of the condominium, including the assignment of limited common elements and general common elements and the respective responsibilities for their maintenance, repair and replacement, and the respective rights of the developer, co-owners and association of co-owners, are contained in the condominium documents, which the developer is responsible to prepare.

The term "condominium documents" typically refers to:

- The "Declaration" (or "Master Deed," as it is referred to in Michigan and in the remainder of this book).

- The "Condominium Bylaws," which are part of the Master Deed and are the basic constitution of how the condominium project will operate and function.

- The "Subdivision Plan," another part of the Master Deed, which locates the condominium unit at a point in space, using surveyor's coordinates.

- The "Articles of Incorporation" or similar document necessary to establish the condominium association as a corporation under the applicable state corporation law.

- The "Corporate Bylaws," sometimes called "Association Bylaws," of the condominium association, which provide for the operation of the association, including details regarding officers, directors, meetings, order of business and so forth.

Sometimes, the Condominium Bylaws and the Association Bylaws are combined in a single document.

The "co-owner," as he or she is frequently referred to when he purchases a condominium unit, becomes a member of an "association of co-owners," or simply the "association" or "condominium association." The association may be any type of legal entity; generally, however, the association of co-owners is a non-profit corporation.

If the association is a corporation, it will have all the vestiges of any other corporation of that type organized in that particular state. Since most corporations have boards of directors or trustees, the association, no doubt, will have a board of directors elected by the members of the association to manage the affairs of the condominium project.

When one takes title to his or her condominium unit, he or she, as a co-owner, becomes a voting member of the association. The weight given the vote of each co-owner as a member of the association is normally determined by the "percentage of value" assigned to his condominium unit in the Master Deed.

Generally, the association will be responsible to govern and maintain the common elements in the condominium project. However, the responsibility to maintain, repair and/or replace the common elements, particularly those which are limited common elements, may not be placed exclusively on the association of co-owners but, rather, in some instances, is imposed upon the individual co-owner(s) themselves.

For instance, while the association generally is responsible to maintain, repair and replace the common elements, each co-owner typically is responsible for the maintenance and upkeep of the interior of his own unit and, perhaps, certain limited common elements assigned to his unit. (In a "site" condominium, the co-owner owns, and generally will be responsible to maintain, repair and replace both his dwelling and the exterior areas of the unit.)

Obviously, your condominium documents must be read carefully to understand which parts of your condominium are designated as units, limited common elements or general common elements, and the extent to which the association is responsible for their maintenance and repair.

The association's management skill and diligence (or lack thereof) may have a significant impact upon its members. Keep in mind that the association is usually responsible for the maintenance of all portions of the condominium, other than the condominium units, such as the hallways, lobbies, building exteriors, landscaping, snow removal, trash pickup and street maintenance (if the roads are private), and for the general operation of the common elements, including the recreational facilities, heating plant, water or electric systems and the like. These tasks often are performed through a management firm, administrator or manager hired by the association board or, in some instances, by the co-owners themselves, if the condominium is "self-managed."

The management company or managing agent, should the nonprofit corporation wish to hire one, is the entity that assists the board of directors in carrying out its responsibilities in managing the affairs of the condominium association. The managing agent may (and, while the developer is in control of the association at the initial stages of the project, typically will) be the developer or an affiliate of the developer.

Beware of situations where the developer is managing the condominium project either directly or through a subsidiary corporation. That frequently results in substantial abuse, which many condominium statutes allow to happen without adequate protections. In Michigan, the condominium association, after the non-developer co-owners obtain the right to elect a majority of the directors, generally can terminate any contracts with the developer that were made while the developer was in control of the association. This includes any long-term management contracts that were entered into with the developer or an affiliate of the developer.

Returning to the association, each co-owner pays a periodic fee, usually monthly, generally referred to as an "assessment," to defray the cost of services rendered by the association. On a yearly basis, the board of directors of the association will determine how much money it will need to run the affairs of the condominium. It then will divide the cost of operation among association members based upon the formula required by the condominium documents. The weight of the co-owner's vote and his financial obligation to support the association may not be the same; typically, however, the percentage of value also is used to determine the percentage of the total assessment, as determined by the budget, one will have to pay to the association on an annual basis.

Special assessments may be made by the board of directors to cover unexpected operational expenditures and repairs; but generally, any substantial increase by way of a special assessment for capital improvements or the like must be approved by a specified vote of the co-owners. Condominium bylaws typically set a dollar or subject matter limit on additional assessments that may be approved by the board of directors without a vote of the co-owners.

Provisions imposing late charges and other penalties for not paying assessments are commonly found in the condominium documents. Additionally, if one mortgages a unit, he may be required to notify the association of the name of the lender who is

holding the mortgage and, after default in the payment of assessments, the association may have to inform the mortgage holder
of any unpaid assessments due for the unit.

What many purchasers do not realize is that many condominium statutes grant to the association a lien against the condominium unit for unpaid assessments. This lien may be foreclosed
in the same way a mortgage holder does after a default in the
payment of mortgage payments. A foreclosure could result in the
forced sale of the unit at public sale or auction and a loss of the
unit to the association or other successful bidder.

The condominium association has a great deal of power, not
only to enforce the documents as they relate to the collection of
assessments, but also to determine how you can live and what
freedoms you have to enjoy your condominium unit and the
project. For instance, there may be restrictions on the use of a
unit that can be enforced by the association. These may include
such things as restrictions on pets, the selling or renting of a unit,
the planting of flowers, posting of signs and the parking of cars.
The association may also have the right to set rules for the use of
the recreational facilities and other common elements. It usually
has the right to require approval of proposed modifications one
may wish to make to the exterior or structural components of his
unit. The subject of restrictions will be discussed in another chapter of this book.

I will also discuss in a subsequent chapter of this book why
it is important that you determine "who's in charge" of the
association. As previously noted, the association is governed by
a board of directors. The developer and/or its designees have
the right to appoint the members of the board of directors who
will run the association until the time prescribed by statute and/
or the condominium documents as the date control of the non-
profit corporation must be turned over to the non-developer co-
owners. This "transition of control" typically takes place after a

sufficient percentage of units in the project have been sold or a certain amount of time has elapsed. During this period, the developer, through his appointees to the board of directors, determines the amount of assessments that will have to be paid by the co-owners in the project. The developer also may be able to amend the condominium documents without the approval of the co-owners, so long as the amendment does not "materially" affect the rights of the co-owners, again dependent upon the respective state enabling statute.

In many respects, a condominium operates as a stand-alone community. In fact, however, the co-owners also must adhere to the zoning and other ordinances of the city or township of which the condominium is a part. Moreover, the condominium may be a part of a larger development, such as a Planned Unit Development (PUD). A PUD is a scheme of development which may include different forms of development—such as some, or all, of a cooperative, a condominium, a traditional subdivision, a recreational facility, a commercial office project and retail space—within a geographic area.

A "community association," as that term is generally used, is an organization established to manage and maintain such a multi-use community. For example, a community association may be formed to manage, provide common services to and maintain architectural control over the PUD, which includes a residential condominium, a retail "strip" mall and commercial office space. Similarly, an "umbrella" community association may provide services, such as administration and maintenance, to a group of subdivisions or condominiums that share the use of roads, utilities or recreational amenities.

While it is not my purpose in this book to provide a legal analysis of the types of entities with which you may become involved when buying a condominium, you should be familiar with all of the types of entities with which you are likely to become legally involved when you buy a condominium unit, ranging from the "umbrella community association" to the developer and management company.

It is the interrelationship between the condominium association, its board of directors, its management agent, if any, and the co-owners that will be the focal point of much of the discussion in the chapters that follow. They will show how you, as a prospective purchaser, present co-owner or board member, can learn to deal with the complexities of these interrelationships.

CHAPTER 2

I Know My Rights...

Understanding State and Federal Statutes and Regulation

As a prospective condominium purchaser or a director of a condominium association, one should at least have a general knowledge of the state and federal statutes and regulations applicable to the condominium.

In many states, first-generation condominium statutes created a regulatory body or agency to administer the sale and development of condominiums. The rationale for involving a state regulatory body is that the sale of a condominium is analogous to a security and that some form of state regulation of its sale is necessary in order to protect the purchaser. In Michigan, for example, the Horizontal Real Property Act of 1963 established powers in an administrator who was an employee of the Michigan Department of Commerce and was assigned the responsibility to review all development and sales documents incidental to the sale of interests in a condominium project by a developer. The developer was required to obtain a permit to sell condominium units before sales transactions could be consummated in the state. The condominium master deed, condominium and association bylaws and sales and advertising materials were required to be approved by the Department of Commerce, Condominium Section, before they could be used by a developer. State administrative regulation of condominiums was intended to ensure that condominium developers adhered to the dictates of the statute, that unreasonable or unconscionable restrictions or provisions were not placed in the condominium documents by unscrupulous developers and their lawyers, and that there was some uniformity in condominium document content.

In general, state regulation of the sale of condominiums worked well. It served as a filtering process to eliminate many bad developers and bad condominium documents. In Michigan, the state regulatory body had a great deal of power to ensure that the developer met commitments made when it sold condominium units—including adequate funding of the condominium association, the completion of promised amenities, and the correction of defects and deficiencies in the condominium project.

Those who opposed state regulation of condominiums complained that the regulatory process was unnecessarily time consuming and expensive for the developer. Others complained that influential developers and/or their lawyers received favored, preferential treatment from state regulators. Still others complained that state regulatory agency approval provided the purchaser a false sense of security concerning the quality and fairness of condominium documents that had received agency approval.

Through a step-by-step process, the Michigan state regulatory body was relieved of most of its pre-sale responsibilities for condominiums. In effect, by 1983 the result was "deregulation" of the sale of condominiums. Most other states also have embraced deregulation. Interestingly enough, Florida and California, which are perhaps the two states with the most condominiums, continue to heavily regulate the sale and development of condominiums.

The sale of residential condominiums has traditionally been a subject of state regulation. Whether condominium deregulation is a good idea is subject to political, as well as legal, debate. Both sides have strong arguments.

The statutes of "deregulated" states give the purchaser or association very little, if any, administrative process recourse against the inexperienced or unscrupulous developer who fails to comply with the basic requirements of the condominium statute and/or basic tenets of fundamental fairness. Redress is left to the courts, which is likely to be both expensive and time consuming.

The suggestion that a purchaser or association may obtain redress by pursuing an action seeking revocation of the developer's builder or real estate broker license is often wishful thinking. Rarely is a developer's builder or real estate broker license revoked, and then only after long, drawn out proceedings that provide the association or disgruntled purchaser a less immediate and effective remedy than is available through the court system.

On the other hand, condominium deregulation has encouraged the development of property, since it can be accomplished more quickly and less expensively than before deregulation. Moreover, the "built-in" protections against developer abuse that are found in most second-generation condominium statutes have proven more effective in curbing developer abuse than many, including I, initially believed.

Developers who meet their responsibilities are flourishing without undue governmental interference under condominium deregulation. However, it is important that such developers play a leadership role in policing their industry. If the excesses of "bad" developers are not voluntarily curbed through industry pressure, an avalanche of anger and protest may erupt when the abuses come to light, with the result that legislatures may "roll back" deregulation to ensure that essential consumer rights are protected. The pendulum may swing back to the regulation of condominiums if developers abuse their prerogatives or if "good" developers fail to police the excesses of "bad" developers.

There are, I fear, thousands of instances in which condominium documents recorded in "deregulated" states are not in conformity with the statute or are of blatantly poor quality. I have seen situations where condominium projects have been expanded beyond the permissible statutory period, or where the subdivision plan drawings required by statute were never prepared or recorded, and, yet, mortgage and title companies lent money and issued title policies for the sale of units. I have seen overbearing, and even unscrupulous, clauses added to condominium documents without objection or outcry by the purchaser or condominium association.

From the perspective of the prospective purchaser or association director, what is important is that they do their "homework" and know exactly their state and local regulatory rights and remedies. The state condominium law may afford remedies, notwithstanding that the state has gone to deregulation. There may be another statute or a municipal ordinance in effect that the developer did not follow. There may be, for example, money which was posted by the developer as a bond to ensure completion, and which is now available to the association or purchasers of a condominium. The local municipality may assist the association by holding back additional building permits until the developer complies with site or code requirements for the units already constructed. Finally, consumer protection laws of more general application may establish the potential for significant civil and, in some instances, criminal penalties.

As a practical matter, you first should determine whether the state or municipality in which you are buying a condominium, or in which the association you serve is located, retains regulatory power over the sale and development of condominiums and the subsequent operation of their associations. Keep in mind that there are states with a loosely defined condominium statute which lacks specific parameters regulating the development of condominiums.

In general, the more statutory law there is in your state, and the more case law concerning the sale and operation of condominiums, the more accurate that the experienced community association practitioner will be in ascertaining the probability of your success against the "bad" developer. The community association practitioner in Florida probably has a better grasp of the law, and consequently the probable result, than does the practitioner in a state where there is no condominium statute, no body of case law and/or no strong state regulatory body.

What also should not be underestimated is that the condominium association, sometimes comprised of hundreds of individuals, has political and economic power. That power should be exerted when dealing with national, state and local agencies. In addition, when condominium associations band together to promote their views on such matters as taxation and community services, they may wield substantial power because of the sheer numbers available to them.

Too often, associations are instead dysfunctional in coordinating their efforts, not only among themselves, but in joining groups to influence particular problems. Fortunately, there are exceptions at both the national and state level.

At the national level, the Community Associations Institute, founded in 1975 and headquartered in Alexandria, Virginia, serves as a catalyst to provide education for all participants in the condominium industry, including developers, managers, public interest officials, condominium professionals and community association organizations.

In Michigan, the United Condominium Owners of Michigan was formed in 1973 to advance the interests of condominiums in the state. While not a lobby group per se, it is a voluntary non-profit organization formed to educate condominium associations and their directors in advancing the interests of condominiums regarding proposals for legislation and general enhancement of condominium living.

The condominium association, developer or purchaser of a condominium should inquire about and support such local, state and national organizations. Developers have tended to gravitate toward organizations such as the local builder's or apartment owner's association to advance their interests. There is a need for organizations to represent all interests involved in the condominium industry. If these organizations are supported and flourish, a better condominium product will result for all concerned!

In suggesting that there are remedies available at the state, local and national level, I emphasize that there are no shortcut answers to resolving the problems of condominium development and living. For example, concerning construction problems, associations and co-owners often have sought a quick-fix remedy in order to avoid the cost and delay of the judicial process and, for that matter, the administrative process. They accept the promises of the developer even though they know all too well, based on the developer's track record, that such promises are not likely to be fulfilled. They may write their congress person, their state legislator, their mayor or the local building inspector to obtain redress. (Sometimes, redress may be obtained through the intervention of the local building official, so I do not mean to discourage exploration of this avenue.)

The aggrieved person usually finds that he is "spinning his wheels" when he seeks redress from a politician who does not have direct jurisdiction or control. Writing your U.S. senator about a roof leak in your condo will more than likely not result in any meaningful resolution of the problem. Although the senator may be kind enough to respond to your letter and direct you to a local consumer protection agency, generally that will not result in an adequate or expeditious resolution of your problem.

It may be that available remedies should be exercised in combination to redress the problem. For example, it may be appropriate to threaten legal proceedings and, at the same time, request state administrative intervention. Similarly, if the local building inspector is sympathetic to the association's plight, he may exert pressure upon the developer to resolve the problems involved. Occasionally, the municipality may intervene in the condominium project to protect the interests of the municipality, which, in turn, may be beneficial to the interest of the purchaser or association. Common sense should enter into the picture when identifying the best remedy available to the association or aggrieved person.

The final point to be made here is that there are a number of remedies available to an aggrieved purchaser or association. You should be aware of all the remedies available, and you should selectively determine, usually with the advice of competent legal advice, the remedy best suited to your situation.

A person residing in a condo and, especially, members of the board of directors and others administering the condo project or assisting the board of directors should also become familiar with certain applicable Federal laws, including, without limitation, the Federal Fair Housing Amendments protecting against discrimination in housing, the Servicemembers Civil Relief Act protecting persons in the military, and the Federal Communications Commission Rules promulgated under the Federal Telecommunications Act of 1996 which protect citizens rights to receive telecommunication reception in their condominium setting, with certain limited restrictions.

CHAPTER **3** | **Condo, Sweet Condo**
Purchasing a Condo as Your
Primary Residence

THE COMMUNAL LIVING MODEL

One who considers condominium living soon recognizes that he must become a student of communal living. Communal living in our society exists in a number of forms. Shared responsibility for the operation of a particular geographic environment is not a unique concept, and the problems of inter-relationships between individuals confined within a geographic boundary also are not unique. Typical examples of communal living range from depersonalized arrangements, such as jails, hospitals, health clubs and country clubs, to personalized living arrangements, such as community associations, PUDs, apartments, residence halls, neighborhood associations, trailer parks, co-housing communities and marina boat parks.

If one wishes to understand the real notion of a condominium, one must be an observer of other types of communal living. To a varying degree, basic precepts of human interplay within an institutional environment, such as a jail, hospital or health club, apply as well to condominium living, insofar as there needs to be limitations on the liberties of persons living in proximity and sharing common facilities.

I have often believed that an exhaustive psychological background in the phenomena of group behavior, particularly as it relates to communal living models, would assist me in dealing with condominiums. People change when they operate in a communal environment. For instance, the collective decision of the board of directors of a condominium association often will not reflect the individual feelings of its members, who, if separately polled on an issue, might reach a different result. (People would likely become more honest about their true feelings or they might become more dictatorial.) They may use the condominium mode of living as an opportunity to lie back and relax, or to release their pent-up aggressions or frustrations. This phenomenon has been confirmed in research discussions with community association practitioners across 50 states. It's clear to me that additional research is needed to explore the phenomenon of condominium living and governance, and to attempt to isolate and interpret the behavioral characteristics that permeate condominium operation.

Some problems of senior housing and assisted living facilities also apply to condominiums, particularly when people are not able to take care of themselves. This becomes an increasing problem as our population ages. The board of directors of a condominium association must struggle with the needs of people that are disabled, physically or mentally infirm or otherwise unable, or unwilling, to live with their neighbors in an unattended, congenial and/or law-abiding manner.

Similarly, the college dormitory is a place of active social interaction, including sexual, educational and recreational. The study of dormitory living, alone, can benefit the researcher analyzing the condominium operation. That some condominium projects include numbers of college students who live there as owners or tenants poses unique problems to the condominium's operation.

The extent to which low-income housing attributes and characteristics apply to the condominium model depends upon the social-economic groups living in the condominium. In a low-income situation, even a modest increase in the assessments can pose serious problems to the co-owners and threaten the successful operation of the condominium association. Too frequently, a person of minimal means purchases a condominium, through subsidy or otherwise, with a minimal or no down payment and without an appreciation of the true costs which will be required to operate and maintain the condominium.

A fundamental question is whether the condominium is suitable as a form of low-income housing. While condominium boards may try to adjust to an increase in their operating costs by spreading needed additional or special assessments over an extended period, some co-owners will not be able to keep up and will either sell or default to the mortgage company or condominium association. In any event, it is clear that the condominium association must remain economically self-sustaining, cannot function as a welfare agency and cannot operate at the level of the lowest common denominator.

I have attempted in this section to introduce issues and point to life situations which are, at least in certain respects, comparable to life in a condominium. However, the answer to the group behavior dynamics of a condominium remains ripe for discussion. Send me your comments at www.meisner-law.com.

IS A CONDO RIGHT FOR ME?

First, a word about the acceptability of condominiums in your locale. Condominiums are not popular everywhere. For example, co-ops are considered to be housing for the affluent in New York, while in other municipalities, co-ops are synonymous with subsidized "low income" housing. Generally, however, condominiums have been accepted for nearly 30 years by both the public and the lending institutions that fund their purchase.

Newspaper ads, TV and radio spots, glossy brochures and even your best friends may extol the virtues of living in a condominium, either as a primary or secondary residence. Advertising jingles and hype create the illusion of the condominium as "care-free living." To the contrary, I have discerned over my years of experiences, both as a counselor to and resident of condominiums, that condominium living is more accurately described as "careful living."

If the prospective purchaser of a condominium learns anything from this book, it should be the importance of adequate preparation and analysis before one buys a condominium. Once the purchase has been made, the purchaser is committed to the condominium "concept," and his choices are limited to the resale or leasing of his unit, or to a change in his personality, philosophy and way of life that will conform to the condominium "concept."

What type of person is suited to condominium living? Perhaps the easiest way to answer the question is to describe the person who is not suited to condominium living.

As previously noted, attached condominium living generally is not suited to large families with young children who will wish to play, dogs who will need to be walked or multiple automobiles that will need to be parked or stored.

Condominium living is not for the person who is used to:

• A farm environment;

• A sprawling, single-family lot; or

- Who, without the permission of "big brother," desires to plant trees, decorate the exterior of his home, put up a large outside satellite dish on a general common element or enlarge the size of his patio or deck.

Condominium living is not for the person who is unwilling to follow restrictions upon the kind of vehicle he may drive, the number of animals he may nurture, the parties he may have, the additional persons who may reside at the condominium and the like. Condominium living also is not for the person who is unwilling to spend large sums of money to maintain the exterior of his home because he does not care how it looks. In short, condominium living is not for the avid supporter of the American Civil Liberties Union! If you wish to live in a condominium, you must be prepared to give up a portion of the liberties, and the flexibility of lifestyle, which you might enjoy in a single-family, detached dwelling. If you are not such a person, you may wish to reconsider the condominium as a form of ownership and mode of living.

Conversely, condominium living may be the perfect answer for the person who wants to increase the amount of property and amenities he can afford by reducing his price per square foot; who wishes to delegate to others the obligations of maintenance, repair and replacement of exterior and common areas; who is willing to abide by restrictions, rules and regulations; and who wishes to enhance his social or recreational opportunities at a minimum cost.

In order to determine whether you are a good candidate for condominium living, you must understand what condominium living is all about. That, of course, requires that you have read this book at least three times; only then will you fully recognize the benefits—and the detriments—of condominium living!

I have assumed that you are planning to reside in your condominium. Condominiums for investment, as well as recreational condominiums, will be discussed in later chapters. If you buy a condominium unit and plan on living in it as your primary residence, you should be reasonably sure that you are going to enjoy living there. Don't forget the basics, including whether you can stand to live with someone living directly above or next to you. While you may have the option to rent out the condominium unit, you should assume when you buy that you will be living there for an indefinite period. Given those considerations, it is essential that you understand the dynamics of condominium living, generally, and of the condominium project you are considering, specifically.

Those of us who are involved in the condominium industry will always agree on at least one thing. The biggest problem in the condominium setting is that condominium purchasers do not know what it's really like to live in a condominium and do not have a clear understanding of what their responsibilities and obligations are, as contained in the condominium documents. For some reason, most condominium owners choose to not read the documents, choose to not secure the assistance of qualified professional advisers who understand and can interpret the documents, or, if they have done so, conveniently forget what they have been told and do not wish to follow.

If, on the other hand, the prospective purchaser does what he is supposed to do to acquaint himself with the facts of condominium living and, in particular, the material facts about the project, not only will he be a more enlightened purchaser and a better condominium resident, but the condominium as a whole will be enhanced by his very presence. There would be one less person who has purchased a condo who has no business living in one!

THE FIRST STEP

What should a person interested in the purchase of a condominium do first? As with any purchase, the purchaser should consider the reasons he or she is considering a condominium and the price he or she can afford to pay. For example, a single person may consider moving to a condominium from an apartment because he or she believes that the time constraints, occasioned by his or her career or school, prevent him or her from caring for a home. Therefore, desiring to build up equity as opposed to paying rent may cause he or she to find the condominium an attractive alternative. It may also give him or her an opportunity to meet other people through the condominium association,which may provide social, recreational, business or even political contacts in the community.

The retiree may look at a condominium as a place he can live in relative comfort, free of the obligation to care for the yard, plow the snow or worry about the repair of the roof. The condominium also may benefit the childless couple that does not have the money to buy a sprawling residence, but wishes to take advantage of the amenities provided by the condominium project, which may include a clubhouse, pool, exercise room or jogging path.

Condominiums come in all locations, sizes and varieties. Location, as with any piece of real estate, is the key to the successful condominium purchase. A particular condominium may be ideal for one couple or single, but not for another couple or single. For example, a high-rise condominium in downtown Detroit may offer the benefits of an urban center to a single person or an appropriate couple, while a townhouse condominium in the affluent Michigan suburb of Bloomfield Hills might be more appropriate to the person who prefers a suburban setting.

Price also will be a factor. Before choosing a particular condominium, the purchaser should consider similar condominiums that are available and compare the cost of single-family homes in the vicinity in which he or she wishes to locate. An additional consideration may be whether to buy "new" from the developer or to purchase a "used" unit in an established or "conversion" condominium project.

The time that you buy into the condominium project, particularly if you are buying from the developer, may have a bearing on the purchase price as well as your decision to buy the unit. For example, if you are living in the apartment building that is about to be converted, you may have rights under state law to preserve your apartment status for a period of time. In some instances, depending upon your age and whether or not you are a person with a disability, this may be a period of years. If so, you may be offered discounts by the developer to buy the condominium unit in which you live. In the case of new construction, you may be offered a pre-construction price that, presumably, will be less than the price at which units will be offered to later purchasers. You also may be offered additional amenities at a reduced price, or without additional charge, or may be given a break on mortgage financing.

Whether you should pay for your unit with cash or borrowed funds depends upon economic considerations that are beyond the scope of this book, other than to suggest that you should consult with your financial planner or investment counselor as to whether it would be more beneficial for you to invest cash in the condominium or to finance it. You should consider factors of inflation, the availability of cash reserves to you, the alternate potential investments that are available to you with the cash that you would use to purchase the condominium, the cost of borrowing money and the credit and psychological ramifications to you of debt, if relevant.

A word about new construction versus "conversion" condominiums is pertinent here. A conversion condo is a project in which the units have been occupied in some form, other than a condominium, before the conversion by the developer. An example would be an apartment building that has been converted into a condominium. The apartment building, obviously, is not new, and is generally sold on an "as is" basis. Beware!

The law in most states, as in Michigan, imposes different responsibilities on the developers of "new construction" and "conversion" condominiums. Over the years, there has been considerable abuse in situations where condominium converters made only cosmetic changes to the existing building and sold the units and common areas "as is," suggesting to their naive purchasers either that there were no serious problems in the condominium project or that they did not know the real condition of the buildings and amenities.

Too often, what has happened is that the purchasers of units later discovered serious problems in the condominium project (particularly the common elements, which the purchaser seldom examines) and found that the association coffers contained inadequate funds to fix them. When the developer hides behind the "as is" disclaimer in its purchase agreement or disclosure statement, the condominium association is faced with raising funds through additional or special assessments before it can repair or replace substantially deteriorated condominium common areas.

Some municipalities have local ordinances that require the developer to provide an inspection report to the purchaser of a conversion project. You should check with your local municipality or state regulatory body to determine whether there are any ordinances that require the developer to provide you with an inspection report concerning the premises.

You should recognize that, while an inspection of the condition of roofs, exterior and structural elements may not reveal current defects, they are not "new" and their remaining useful life may be in question. For instance, roofs that may have been on for 15 years may fail within a few years, and there may be insufficient funds set aside in reserve to replace them.

In the case of a conversion condominium, it is vital that the purchaser understand that, although local building authorities may have inspected the building's heating, plumbing and electrical systems, together with its roofing and structural supports, the inspection generally will not include a determination of the condition of other elements of the project. Additionally, it is important to remember that a local building authority inspection (if any is required) of a conversion condominium may only apply the construction codes that were in effect at the time the structure was originally erected or remodeled. If so, building authority approval of the building may provide no assurance that the building conforms to the current construction codes. (Any extensive remodeling done at the time of conversion, however, generally must meet current construction standards.)

The developer generally does not assume responsibility for the project when it is offered "as is." Consequently, you need to personally inspect not only the condominium unit you wish to purchase, but the condition of the buildings and other common portions of the condominium in order to determine their adequacy and condition.

In the conversion condo, the developer may be expected to provide you with a "Disclaimer of Warranties," wherein it attempts to reaffirm that the condominium project is being sold "as is, where is;" that there are no warranties, express or implied, of any kind made with regard to pre-existing building elements; and that the purchaser may be required to contribute substantial sums of money for condominium association assessments for the repair and replacement of common elements at some future time. Unfortunately, most prospective purchasers never really understand or comprehend this language, or perhaps they never even read it. This is exacerbated by the fact that the selling broker, typically, is telling the condominium purchaser how cheap it will be to live in the condominium project; how the developer is honorable and has had years of experience in converting condos;

how beautiful the grass has been manicured and the how nice the streets look (has the developer put an asphalt blacktop coat over a concrete road with material subsurface defects?); and that the advertised assessment should be more than adequate to fund the reserves, particularly since the developer has already contributed $5,000 for that purpose!

In Michigan, a developer of a conversion condominium is obligated to disclose the physical condition of the condominium if he knows it. Many developers claim in the disclosure statement that they do not know. If you see that statement, BEWARE!

New construction, of course, has its own problems. With any new construction, one normally should expect that there will be certain problems. While the law generally implies warranties regarding habitability and fitness of the condominium units and common elements, developers generally will limit their economic exposure by placing limits on the extent, scope and duration of the warranty they provide to purchasers. Typically, a one-year warranty is given to a purchaser, which is really not an awful lot of time to determine the scope and magnitude of the problems that may be latent in the construction of the project.

One minor advantage to a conversion condominium may be that the buildings have been inspected by the developer (or by an engineer hired by the developer to survey the major component parts of the project, assuming that he has truthfully and fully disclosed the condition of same) and many of the initial construction "bugs" have been discovered and, presumably, corrected. In new construction, the developer may have done an admirable job in building the units, if the units are there to observe. However, the condominium may not be totally complete when you consider buying. You may be faced with construction traffic and debris for three or four years while the remainder of the condominium project is completed and all bugs are corrected.

In a conversion condominium, the units generally will have

been refurbished and will be available for occupancy immediately. In a new construction condominium, the developer may construct units in phases, for various reasons, including economic and legal, and you may be subjected to delays before your particular unit is completed.

After careful deliberation, you may decide that you would prefer to buy a "resale" condominium, rather than purchase a unit from the developer of a "new construction" or "conversion" project. Even if this is the case, you should investigate the history of the condominium project, that is, was it "new construction" or a "conversion" when it was established? Simply put, the more you know about the history of the development, the happier you will be, assuming you have made a reasonable business decision to buy a condominium in the first place and the condominium that you buy is the one for you!

If you buy a condominium from a developer, you generally will benefit from the protections afforded by state statute and/or the common law to the initial purchasers of condominium units, even in a state that has "deregulated" the development and sale of new condominiums. Conversely, for a resale condominium, there probably will be no state statutory law specific to the sale of condominiums, although general statutes or bodies of case law that would apply to the reseller of any residential real estate will apply.

Occasionally, brokers will insert a provision in a purchase agreement for a "resale" condominium that obligates the purchaser to reimburse the seller for his so-called "owner's equity" in the condominium and/or condominium association. Presumably, the provision contemplates that the condominium owners have built up some equity over the years to which the co-owner of the unit being sold is entitled to a portion, in proportion to the percentage interest assigned to his unit in the Master Deed. Since the co-owner typically cannot seek a refund from the association of his share of the owners' equity, because it is treated as a part of the undivided ownership interest of the co-owner in the unit and common areas, there is no reason why there should be any proration or adjustment of owner's equity in a resale purchase agreement. Rather, the fair market value of the condominium unit purchased should reflect the value of the cubicle of space being sold, the seller's undivided interest in the common areas and the financial condition of the condominium association. The purchaser, therefore, should not allow the broker, who may have drafted the purchase agreement as agent on behalf of the seller, to provide for any type of proration of owner's equity unless the condominium documents specifically authorize the reimbursement of owner's equity to the seller. In that case, there will then be some reasonable basis to prorate the equity between purchaser and seller.

In summary, when looking at condominium units, you should consider the factors discussed in this chapter to help you decide whether you have the "aptitude" to buy a:

- New unit from the developer,

- Conversion unit from the developer,

- Used unit in what was a "new construction" project, or

- Used unit in what was a "conversion" project.

IT'S LIKE FINDING THE RIGHT MATE

Now that you have some idea as to the location in which you desire to purchase, and whether you will consider some, or all, of new, conversion and resale condominiums, you are ready to locate a real estate broker who has had experience in buying and selling condominium units in the locale in which you are interested. A knowledgeable real estate broker should have insight into the better quality condominiums that are available. He should help you to spot those condominium projects that are better managed, and in which the units have appreciated with regularity. A real estate broker also may know of available new construction and may have some idea of the "track record" of the developer.

You also should check local newspaper advertisements and/or the Internet for condominiums, and you may wish to talk to friends and acquaintances who know of existing condominiums that will soon be on the market. But an additional word of caution! If, after reading this book three times as prescribed, you still have no perception of what condo living is about, you should make an appointment with a condominium attorney who should spend at least an hour answering any questions you may have concerning the condominium concept, and especially whether you are a person who should contemplate buying a condo!

YOU MEAN I WILL OWN *THAT*, TOO?

Perhaps the most common error of the prospective condominium purchaser is the failure to understand that a purchaser will buy not only the cubicle of space in which he will live, but also an undivided interest in the common elements of the project. Even though the condominium unit under consideration may be the home of his dreams, the intelligent purchaser will appreciate that he ultimately will be responsible for a portion of the costs of maintenance, repair, and/or replacement of all common areas of the condominium for which the condominium association has responsibility. Consequently, his inspection will not be limited to the condominium unit but will encompass the condominium as a whole.

For example, if the roofs of buildings in a distant portion of the condominium project are deteriorating and the condominium documents provide that the association is responsible for the maintenance of the roofs (as is usually the case), the fact that your own roof is in good condition and will not soon leak may not mean that your investment in the condominium project will be a good one. The association may be required to levy substantial special or additional assessments to defray the cost to replace the roofs at the other end of the project. Or, if the roofs were defectively constructed by the developer and the right to sue has not expired, the association may start a lawsuit against the developer, which, potentially, may cost tens of thousands of dollars to prosecute.

THE CONTRACT

The following discussion of Michigan law and practice is presented by way of illustration only. Of course, you should check with your condominium lawyer as to the particular statutes and common law of your state regarding pre-construction agreements.

In Michigan, the Condominium Act prescribes many of the rights and responsibilities of a condominium developer. Assuming you have located a "new construction" condominium unit that you want to buy, but which is not yet constructed, you may be asked to sign a reservation agreement.

The typical reservation agreement reserves the particular unit you have selected (assuming that you later elect to go ahead with the transaction), in consideration of which you give the developer a deposit as assurance that you are a serious purchaser. The Condominium Act requires that the deposit be held, generally, by a title company or bank, in escrow, pending your final decision to buy the unit.

Typically, a reservation agreement is absolutely binding on neither the developer nor the prospective purchaser. The developer will include various "escape clauses" in the reservation agreement, particularly if the developer decides not to develop the condominium project or to construct the particular unit. Similarly the purchaser may withdraw from a reservation agreement, and recover his deposit, at any time before the unit is established in the master deed and the purchaser signs a purchase agreement.

Later the purchaser of a new construction condominium will be asked to sign a binding purchase agreement.

BEFORE YOU SIGN

In Michigan, the purchase agreement only becomes binding after the purchaser has been given an opportunity to review the condominium documents that will control the operation and development of the condominium project and have been recorded in the public records of the county where the condominium project is located.

Never sign a binding real estate purchase agreement without first seeking the advice of legal counsel, unless the binding effect of the purchase agreement is expressly contingent upon your attorney's subsequent review and satisfaction with its contents!

Such is certainly true in the context of a condominium. For example, in Michigan, when the developer asks that you replace the non-binding reservation agreement with a binding purchase agreement, the developer also must provide you a number of additional documents, and the time in which to review them, before the purchase agreement becomes binding. Those documents which the developer of a Michigan condominium must provide a purchaser include the:

- Master Deed, Condominium Bylaws and Subdivision Plan;

- Articles of Incorporation and Association Bylaws of the non-profit condominium association (the Condominium Bylaws and Association Bylaws may be combined);

- Rules and regulations, if any, of the condominium association that may have been promulgated by the developer;

- Disclosure Statement, a plain-English description of the condominium project prepared by the developer (which will be discussed in greater detail later in this book); and,

- Condominium Buyers Handbook, a publication presently published by the Michigan Department of Labor and Economic Growth designed to acquaint readers with some of the basic aspects of condominium living.

Although the Condominium Buyers Handbook certainly is no substitute for this book (you may have noticed by now that I have discarded all pretense at humility), it does serve to open the eyes of prospective purchasers to some of the pitfalls and problems in buying a condominium, and should be thoroughly read.

In Michigan, a purchase agreement typically contains such elements as the purchase price, terms, legal description of the unit and condominium project, description of any assigned carports, boat wells, parking spaces, etc., and description of conditions of, and remedies after, default. There also are certain legally mandated provisions that a developer must include in the purchase agreement when selling a residential condo unit in Michigan. First, the developer must give the purchaser at least nine (9) business days from the date that he receives the Condominium Documents to determine whether he desires to withdraw from the purchase.

This right to withdraw must be set forth in the purchase agreement, although it can be waived by a prospective purchaser. This "cooling-off" period should never be waived unless the purchaser already is fully acquainted with the condominium and condominium documents and is certain he wishes to go ahead with the purchase arrangement. You should, of course, find out whether your own state law provides for a similar cooling-off period, and, if so, determine the time period prescribed.

A Michigan condominium purchase agreement also must contain provisions for the escrow of deposits, notice of the purchaser's exclusive right to arbitrate any dispute between the purchaser and the developer, provided that the amount at issue is less than $2,500, and of the association's exclusive right to arbitrate any dispute between the association and the developer, provided that the amount at issue is less than $10,000.

The State of Michigan no longer regulates the contents of the Purchase Agreement. Consequently, in Michigan, as in any other state which has "deregulated" its condominium law, a purchaser should have an experienced condominium attorney review the Purchase Agreement to insure that the developer has complied with the dictates of the statute and that the Purchase Agreement is otherwise reasonable, enforceable and properly and clearly sets forth the arrangement that has been struck. At a minimum, a Purchase Agreement should set forth:

- The unit number you are purchasing;

- The price you are paying;

- Any conditions regarding installment payments on the purchase price;

- Your obligation to pay assessments to the condominium association as well as an initial working capital deposit and perhaps contributions towards the insurance reserve and reserve for major repair and replacement;

- The cancellation rights of the purchaser (usually limited to the period before the agreement becomes binding);

- The cancellation rights, if any, of the developer;

- Warranty provisions and guarantees, if any;

- The "fact" that the purchaser may not rely on oral representations; and,

- Provisions governing the rights and responsibilities of the parties after a default by the purchaser or developer.

You should make a point to ask your condominium developer to commit to the date when your unit will be ready for occupancy, particularly if it has not been constructed. The time when it is available not only profoundly affects when you will be willing to leave your present residence, whether it be your current home or an apartment, but also when you will be able to get financing and for how long. Generally, mortgage companies will give commitments for a minimum of 60 days and no longer than six months.

Sometimes the developers and builders of condominiums and single-family homes don't deliver the unit or house as promised. Most developers will give themselves, legally, at least a year to build a condominium unit while holding your funds in escrow. You may or may not be willing to wait that long. And, of course, the Purchase Agreement generally will exclude delays caused by strikes, acts of God, or other emergencies beyond the control of the developer. Try to get the developer to commit to a "time certain" that is no more than six months from the time that you sign the Purchase Agreement—unless you are completely flexible about moving into the unit whenever the developer has it ready and if "locking in" an interest rate on a mortgage is not an issue.

In the case of a conversion condominium, the unit should be ready for occupancy unless the developer is undertaking a substantial refurbishing of the condominium project, in which case you should also be concerned about when the unit will be available for occupancy.

The purchase agreement used for the sale of a condominium by a developer may differ substantially from that used in a "resale" situation. In Michigan, a "resale" purchase agreement is not regulated by any statutory provisions that relate specifically to condominiums. Nevertheless, good legal practice dictates that a purchase agreement for a resale condominium contain all customary provisions that define and protect the rights and obligations of the purchaser and seller of residential property (inclusive of a seller's disclosure statement), generally, and additional provisions unique to the condominium concept, such as:

● Protection for the proration of assessments of condominium units;

● A statement assigning responsibility for additional or special assessments which may be levied;

● Disclosure whether there are any assessments that have been levied but will not be due by the time of closing;

● Provisions for the removal of any contingencies which may be contained in the condominium documents, such as a "right of first refusal" of the condominium association or certain co-owners, or any other restraint on alienation which must be waived; and,

● Assurance that the condominium premises are being sold in a proper and workmanlike condition.

Before signing any purchase agreement, you should consult with your prospective lender as to the length of any commitment it will give you. You may also wish to inquire of your real estate agent or the developer concerning the availability of financing the condominium unit that you are considering. Sometimes a developer will arrange better-than-market-rate mortgages with a local financial institution(s), based upon the volume of units to be sold or because the developer has "bought down" the mortgage, that is, reduced the interest rate or points required to be paid.

The disclosure statement required by the Michigan Condominium Act is an extremely valuable tool for review by the purchaser and his legal counsel. A developer is required in the disclosure statement to disclose material information about the development of the condominium project, relevant information concerning the operation of the association and the history and background of the developer. The disclosure statement, which is vaguely akin to a prospectus for a new stock offering, must include:

● The nature of the units constructed or proposed to be constructed;

● How large the condominium project may become;

● How long the developer has to enlarge or contract the project;

● Whether recreational facilities have to be constructed and, if so, under what conditions;

● The identity of the developer and, if the developer is a corporation, joint venture, partnership, etc., the identity of its principals;

● Whether the developer has had any prior experience in developing condominiums and, if so, where and when;

● Whether there are any pending legal and/or administrative proceedings against the developer that relate to the project;

- What will be expected of the purchaser in regard to his responsibilities as a co-owner (including a brief summary of the restrictions attributable to the condominium project);

- Whether the roads and sewers of the condominium project will be private or public, and

- Any "other unique and/or material aspects of the condominium project that should be disclosed to prospective purchasers," such as warranties or any disclaimer of warranties.

There usually will be attached to the disclosure statement a copy of a proposed budget for the condominium association, which should give the prospective purchaser an inkling of what he will have to pay in assessments to the condominium association.

Careful scrutiny of the budget frequently will result in the conclusion that the budget has been understated, or that it is based upon units in the condominium project that have not, as yet, been established, or may never be established in the exercise of the developer's discretion in expanding the condominium project.

The developer may intentionally underestimate the actual cost to operate the association; remember, a high "maintenance fee" may be an impediment to sales. This practice is referred to as "low-balling" and, unfortunately, historically was a serious problem in the sale of condominium units. With the increased disclosure requirements of the so-called "second-generation" state statutes, developers now can be more readily held accountable for any intentional misrepresentation of the financial ability of the association to satisfy its needs, as reflected in the anticipated budget prepared by the developer.

Keep in mind that the disclosure statement must be updated periodically by the developer. When you are contemplating buying a condominium unit, you should ask the developer whether this is the latest disclosure statement, when it was prepared and whether there have been any material changes of the facts set forth in the disclosure statement. You may even wish to have the developer confirm that fact in writing.

Also keep in mind that the disclosure statement will include disclaimers of oral representations made by the developer and/or its sales agents. A bright "red flag" should appear before your eyes whenever a sales representative tells you that you should not worry about any statement set forth in the purchase agreement or condominium documents! While the law may give you some support, if you intend to rely upon oral representations that contradict the express terms of the purchase agreement or any of the condominium documents, those statements should be reduced to writing before you sign the purchase agreement.

The developer also may disclose in its disclosure statement the form of management under which the condominium association will operate. Consider whether the association is being managed by a professional management company and, if so, whether the professional management company is a subsidiary of the developer or whether it is an outside management company that has no direct affiliation with the developer.

The significance of whether the developer is the managing agent of the condominium association may have some bearing on whether the developer has had prior experience in managing condominiums and whether the developer is sincere in trying to establish a condominium association which will be well-run, not only in its initial stages, but also after the association has been turned over to the co-owners.

In short, the disclosure statement can be a valuable source of information to you and your attorney. It can serve as a source reference to gain additional insight and information about the developer's present and future plans for the condominium project and its experiences in past condominiums.

If the developer discloses the names of condominiums that it has developed or with which it has been affiliated, if it has had such experience, you or your attorney should inquire of the officers and directors of those associations as to the experiences they have had with the developer.

In a resale condo, your state may have a separate "seller disclosure statement" requirement that applies generally to any residential resale situation, and requires disclosure of common element problems, such as in Michigan.

The more you know about the developer before you buy, the more enlightened your purchase will be. That will be a recurring theme in this book and you will be glad that you remembered it if you buy a condominium unit.

4 | Location, Location, Location
Purchasing a Condo as an Investment

In a sense, everyone who buys a condominium or any other type of real estate is making an investment. While the investor's primary purpose may be to find a suitable place to live, the purchaser normally expects that his or her home will appreciate, at a minimum, at the current rate of inflation. A condominium also can be purchased as an investment, without the expectation that it will be occupied as one's primary residence. This chapter will focus on the various types of condominiums and consider, briefly, which can be considered a potentially good investment.

SECOND HOME VS. INVESTMENT PROPERTY

We'll first discuss the purchase of a condominium as a second home, either as a pure investment or as an outlet for recreational activities.

Regardless of tax ramifications, from a purely financial standpoint, a condominium as a recreational or second home may be a good investment, dependent upon the location of the condominium, its proximity to the investor, the facilities offered and the like. The cash flow generated by a condominium which is not used as the primary home of the investor frequently does not meet the actual expenses incurred in operating and maintaining the condominium, including debt service, assessments and taxes, insurance and rental management fees. However, when appreciation and certain favorable tax advantages also are considered, investment in a residential condo may well prove beneficial.

Second home condos have been extremely popular in certain areas of the country. Florida, for example, has seen the greatest development of condos as second homes. Many owners of Florida condos are residents of other states, particularly in the Northeast and Midwest. A "second home" condominium in Florida, California, Colorado or another so-called "prime" recreational location continues to be a good investment, but the investor should use good common sense and adhere to the criteria outlined in other places in this book.

THE COMMERCIAL CONDOMINIUM

The potential of the commercial condominium is only now being recognized. Initially, the commercial condominium seems to have found its greatest acceptance in Southern California.

Commercial condominiums may take the form of office buildings, warehouses, industrial parks or storage facilities. They make economic sense to the investor—usually a corporation, limited partnership or limited liability company—that does not find it appropriate to pay rent and expects to benefit from the potential for appreciation in value.

A potential problem for the investor in a commercial condominium is the limitation that is inherently imposed upon it regarding the space purchased. For example, the doctor who buys an office suite in a commercial condominium may later run out of space and be unable to expand—unless there are convertible areas or he has reserved the right to buy additional space from the condominium developer, the association or other co-owners in the project. The investor who makes a wrong business decision may experience that "boxed in" feeling!

The commercial condominium may be an excellent investment opportunity for the right investor. On the other hand, it always is easier to walk away when one's property is rented rather than owned.

Many state condominium statutes impose fewer restrictions on a commercial condominium than on a residential condominium. One should check the particular state involved to determine the requirements imposed upon the developer and the condominium association concerning the creation, operation and management of the commercial condominium project.

Commercial condominiums share some of the same risks as residential condominiums. Proper management, as well as a spirit of community participation and cooperation, is indispensable. In the commercial condominium, an investor should examine the documents of the project to determine if they provide adequate flexibility to meet the future needs of the potential co-owner or tenant. Flexibility should exist for the expansion or contraction of the size of the condominium unit purchased, the maintenance of common facilities and the division of the costs of operation of the condominium association.

MOBILE HOME CONDOMINIUMS

Although it may be financially more lucrative for the experienced mobile home operator to retain ownership and lease the pads, both the inexperienced operator and the operator who wishes to avoid the day-to-day landlord/tenant aspects of the mobile home community (while retaining, where appropriate and legal, the right to manage the mobile home park for the benefit of the mobile home condominium association) may wish to consider the development and sale of mobile home condominium communities, or the conversion of existing mobile home parks to condominium. The "economics" will dictate whether such an investment is feasible. As with all real estate investments, the most important factor always is "location, location, location."

With the benefit of careful drafting of the mobile home community documents, the mobile home community can be a viable place in which to live and invest. The condominium documents should give the condominium association the latitude and powers necessary to effectively address the unique problems of the mobile home community.

The conversion mobile home condominium has not been widely accepted. The market for mobile homes is composed primarily of lower income individuals who lack sufficient equity to invest in a typical residential community. Similarly, the inherently "transient" nature of the mobile home occupant may make management by a mobile home condominium association more difficult than management by a mobile home operator who may simply evict the tenant who violates the rules and regulations. Finally, the multiplicity of regulations governing the sale of mobile homes is likely to be a deterrent to conversion.

Many state condominium statutes contain provisions that are unique to mobile home condominiums. In Michigan, for example, the developer of a mobile home condominium can sell individual mobile home lots, together with an undivided interest in a community facility.

CAMPSITE CONDOMINIUMS

As with the mobile home condominium, the campsite condo involves the purchase of a plot of land, or envelope of space, within a campsite community, sometimes containing electrical hookups for recreational vehicles within the unit. Typically, ownership of a "campsite" may include a recreational facility, which offers recreational equipment complementary to campsite use.

Again, dependent upon the location and price of the campsite facility, an investment in a campsite condominium may be beneficial, particularly when the investor contemplates permanent and frequent personal use. However, one should carefully evaluate the availability of, and the responsibility to obtain and maintain, water, utilities and improvements.

There are unique problems to campsite condos that must be addressed in the condominium documents. The demarcation of the site from a physical standpoint may pose problems—not only for the developer but also for the purchaser. Adequate maintenance and management of the campsite condo is also extremely important. Finally, although the adequacy of restrictions upon the leasing of sites may be a problem in any residential community, this appears to be particularly true in the context of campsite and mobile home parks.

RETAIL AND HOTEL CONDOMINIUMS

Mixed-use condominiums are growing rapidly in popularity, particularly in urban locations. The mixed-use condo typically is a high-rise building that may include retail and entertainment space, commercial office space and residential apartments. The availability of retail and entertainment services in immediate proximity to one's home may be particularly attractive to the young, single, urban professional, who may enhance his or her ability to balance the time demands of work, play and home. Similarly, the developer of a mixed-use condominium who has no interest in the traditional leasing business may find that the mixed-use retail condominium enhances the value of all components of his project.

It is hard to imagine a retailer buying retail condominium

space in an office building or "strip" center without first ascertaining the desirability of the project and location. A retail condominium may be a sensible investment if the business location is independently attractive and the customer base enhanced by the proximity of residential condominium occupants. When these conditions are satisfied, the retailer's ability to avoid the payment of rent and to share in the presumed appreciation of the project will constitute the "icing on the cake."

As has been previously discussed in the commercial condominium context, the needs of the retail establishment may change, either downward or upward. The retailer must recognize that the marketability of condominium space may be inferior to the marketability of rental space. The investor may be "locked in" to the purchased retail space without the ability to reduce his fixed costs, or alternatively, may be unable to expand to meet new needs or opportunities—in either case to the detriment of his business.

Hotel condominiums generally are found in portions of the country that attract vacationers. Miami Beach is a haven for hotel condominiums. Many hotel condominiums are offered as "time-share" condos, whereby the investor actually purchases the right to use a hotel room or suite and the associated hotel facilities for a fixed number of weeks or days during the year.

From an investment standpoint, a developer who buys a hotel and converts it into a hotel or time-share condominium can, dependent upon the usual factors of location and price, obtain an excellent return on his investment. Time-share condos could take an entire chapter of this book. Suffice it to say that time sharing has been abused by many developers, and many purchasers fail to understand the actual concept of buying into a time-share condominium.

Simply stated, a hotel or time-share condominium will be a risky investment if the investor is not prepared to use the condo on a frequent basis, or if the investor fails to ensure that the leasing of the hotel condo throughout the year is viable and makes economic sense. If possible, the investor ought to invest in a hotel or time-share condo that offers the option to exchange the room with similar rooms in hotels located in other parts of the world.

As with any other type of used real estate, the purchaser must be aware of the physical condition of the premises prior to purchase. The developer should be prepared to adequately disclose the condition of the premises and make the necessary renovations to put the converted condominium hotel in proper condition.

The developer of a hotel condominium should be advised of the legal and business consequences of doing so and should retain the services of a lawyer with expertise in the sub-specialty of condominium hotel development. Moreover, the prospective purchaser of a hotel or time-share condominium interest should closely examine the condominium documents before investing.

PARKING LOT CONDOMINIUMS

The parking lot condominium is well suited to the basketball and football fan who purchases season tickets for his favorite team each year and wishes to park close to the stadium. Simply stated, the investor in a parking lot condo buys a premium parking lot space near an office complex or recreational or sports facility. While parking lot condos are relatively new, I believe they will be highly successful, particularly since parking spaces in major downtown communities around the country are limited and their rental extremely expensive. This would appear to be an area of considerable opportunity for the condominium investor. But, again, the management of the parking facility and enforcement of its restrictions is extremely important.

MARINA CONDOMINIUMS

Marina condominiums are well established as an investment opportunity. As with parking lots, boat slips are hard to find in prime locations. The condominium marina developer may realize an excellent investment return by selling the boat slips but maintaining the management responsibilities (when permitted by local law) and/or services to the marina.

A marina condominium investment can be lucrative for the boat owner, or even for the person who expects to buy a boat at some later time but desires to rent his boat slip in the interim. The investor who buys a marina boat slip does not have to worry that one may not be available for his boat. Moreover, the value of the boat slip is likely to appreciate due to the scarcity of prime boat slip locations and facilities.

This is not to say that marina condominiums are without problems. The boat slip condominium developer should have obtained the proper clearances from federal and state agencies and otherwise comply with state and federal laws regarding the division of water rights. The proper engineering of seawalls and "catwalks" should be confirmed, and not assumed, by the prospective purchaser. As with all condominiums, the documentation for the marina condominium should be properly prepared and the purchase price reasonable.

In summary, condominiums take various forms, and inventive developers and their attorneys are likely to devise new and ingenuous uses of the condominium concept in the future. The condominium offers a viable alternative to leasing for those who would prefer to own, rather than rent, real estate. Perhaps when the sequel to this book is written, there will be condominiums in outer space or under water (by design). Perhaps future space transports will contain a retail condominium. In any event, the opportunities for condominium investment and development are only limited by state law and the imagination of man.

CHAPTER 5

The Best of Both Worlds
Vacation Homes and Taxes

Our review of the condominium as an investment would be incomplete if I failed to mention the tax ramifications of condominium investment. Of particular significance is the so-called "vacation condominium," which typically is a condo used as a secondary residence or investment, and not for homestead occupancy.

The treatment of vacation condominiums under the Internal Revenue Code is similar to the treatment afforded a house, apartment, mobile home, boat or similar property. There are specific limitations on the allowable business deductions available to a taxpayer who uses a vacation home for both personal and rental purposes. These limitations apply to individuals, S-corporations, partnerships, trusts and estates. The number of days that a vacation home is used for personal purposes, as compared to the number of days that the property is rented at fair value, determines the availability of tax deductions.

As of the date of publication of this book, these rules may be summarized as follows:

- Rule No. 1: If the vacation condominium is used by the taxpayer for personal purposes for not more than fourteen (14) days during the taxable year, or for ten percent (10%) of the number of days that it is rented at a fair price (if this is greater), then it is not considered the taxpayer's "home." In this case, tax deductions attributable to income derived from the rental of the property are not limited to gross income produced by the property.

- Rule No. 2: If the personal use of the vacation condominium exceeds the greater of: (a) fourteen (14) days; or (b) ten percent (10%) of the number of days during the taxable year that it is rented at a fair price, then it is considered the taxpayer's "home." In such cases, the tax deductions attributable to income derived from the rental of the property can not exceed the gross income generated by the property.

- Rule No. 3: If the vacation condominium is the taxpayer's "home," and is rented for fewer than fifteen (15) days during the tax year, any income derived from the rental during the tax year is not taxable, but the deductions attributable to income derived from the rental of the property are not allowed (the usual personal deductions for mortgage, interest and real estate taxes, however, may be taken).

- Rule No. 4: If the vacation condominium is not the taxpayer's "home," as described under the vacation home rules, but the rental use is not an activity from which the taxpayer expects to make a profit, the taxpayer's deductible rental expenses may not exceed his rental income, in the same manner as they are limited for a "home" under the vacation home rules. However, if the rental results in a profit during three (3) or more years during a period of five (5) consecutive tax years, it is presumed by the IRS to be an activity engaged in "for profit."

In all cases, except the situation described in Rule No. 3, the personal use of the vacation property, on even a single day, requires that investment expenses be allocated between personal and rental use based on the number of personal days and the number of rental days. The allocation between personal and rental expense is calculated, usually, in the following ratio:

<u>Days rented at a fair rental price</u>
Days of total use

According to the IRS, "Days of total use" equals the number of days the property was rented at a fair rental price plus the number of days of personal use. "Days rented at a fair rental price" is the number of days the property was rented at a fair rental price, excluding any day that the taxpayer also personally used the home. Days that the vacation home is vacant (even if the home is being advertised for rent at a fair rental value) and days spent maintaining the home are not included as days of personal use.

What constitutes "personal use?" The taxpayer is deemed to have used his vacation home for "personal use" for the entire day, even if it is used for only a part of that day, in any of the following instances:

1. If the taxpayer, a member of his family or any person who has an interest in the home uses it for any part of the day, it is a "personal use" day. Family includes the spouse, brothers,

sisters, lineal descendants and ancestors of the taxpayer. However, if the family member rents the vacation property for a fair price for use as his principal residence on that day, this use is not considered "personal use" by the taxpayer. However, if the taxpayer stays at the home while renting it to a family member who is using it as a principal residence, the days that the taxpayer spends at the vacation home count as days of "personal use" by the taxpayer, regardless of the rental agreement.

2. If the vacation home is used by an individual under an arrangement that enables the taxpayer to use some other unit (whether or not fair rental is charged for the use of the other house), the taxpayer is considered to have used the vacation home for "personal use." Thus, a house-swapping arrangement, under which two homeowners rent each other's home as a personal residence, is "personal use" by each taxpayer.

3. Unless a fair rental is received, any period of rental of a vacation home is considered to be "personal use" by the taxpayer.

It generally is to the taxpayer's advantage to avoid having a dwelling unit classified as his "home," because it would subject rental deductions to the gross rent loss limitation. Therefore, most tax planning strategies involve controlling the variables of the fixed formula: rental days and personal days.

Unless an individual rents a unit for less that fifteen (15) days, he or she would be wise to rent it at a fair rental price for as many days as possible (assuming a rental loss) since doing so will increase the number of personal use days a taxpayer can have before the loss limitation applies. To avoid having a vacation condominium classified as the taxpayer's "home," he should carefully plan the number of days it is used for personal purposes during the tax year. The fewer the number of personal use days, the less likely the chance that the vacation condominium can be classified as the taxpayer's "home."

In summary, if a vacation condominium is used solely by the owner for personal purposes, the mortgage interest and taxes are allocable as itemized deductions, but other expenses, such as utilities, repairs, depreciation and rent paid on the home cannot, in most instances, be deducted. The tax ramifications of a vacation home bought strictly as a business investment are equally uncomplicated. When an individual enters into a business venture for the sole purpose of producing income, these deductions are allowed (for example, a rental property leased to others at a fair rent is eligible for tax deductions). When a dwelling unit is used for both personal and business purposes, mortgage interest and taxes will still be deductible and the rules, while more complex, may still permit the deduction of other expenses, to the extent allocated to the days rented. An understanding of these rules can aid taxpayers in making prudent tax decisions regarding vacation homes. You are advised to seek advice from a competent tax consultant of your choice before making any purchase.

CHAPTER 6 Closing Time
Guidelines for Selling a Condo

Initially, following the introduction of condominiums in the 1960s, the market for the resale of condominiums was a seesaw affair. There was the difficulty in recognizing condominiums as a viable form of ownership appropriate for the investor, including the person who wished to live in the condominium as his primary residence. Sure, co-ops had been accepted in the eastern United States, where many financial institutions had no trouble financing them. On the other hand, the co-op had a bad reputation in certain other parts of the country, where it had become synonymous with low-income housing.

In the 1960s and 1970s, condominiums were the "new kid on the block." Most financial institutions were skeptical of them. Add to that scenario the horror stories from Florida, where unscrupulous developer abuses included the "low-balling" of assessments, shoddy workmanship and inequitable recreational leases. As a result, there developed a general disdain for condominium in many parts of the country.

With the passage of time, condominiums gained acceptance and are now not only accepted but are glamorized by Hollywood. John Paxton wrote a song about condos and yuppies. Condos for the vacation home-rental market have flourished in Ft. Lauderdale, Aspen, Naples, Dana Point, Palm Beach and South Beach. High-rise condos are a hot item, particularly in New York, Chicago and Washington, D.C.

SELLING GUIDELINES

In this chapter we will consider guidelines for the seller of a residential condominium. We will assume that the person selling the condominium is not desperate to do so, notwithstanding that he may have served on the board of directors, may have contracted "condominium depression" or may have been persecuted by the condominium association. We also will assume that he is not motivated to sell by his refusal to adhere to rules and regulations or because he has been embarrassed by the condo association in its efforts to compel compliance. Moreover, we will assume that he is not desperate to sell because the condominium association has failed to fix his roof and he has, both literally and figuratively, "thrown in the towel."

We are, rather, assuming that the co-owner is selling his unit for a reason having nothing to do with the condominium itself, is willing to comply with the requirements of state law and the condominium documents when selling the unit, and will exercise sound judgment and business practices in his effort to obtain the best price for the unit.

When a person sells a condominium unit, he must first determine how he will list the unit for sale. Many condominium documents prohibit the posting of signs concerning the sale of a condominium unit. You should check with your condominium association to determine its current policy, if any, in that respect. Such restrictions may impair your ability to sell "By Owner."

Remember, however, that even if signs are permitted, you may benefit from the assistance of a professional real estate broker in selling your unit. In all probability, a professional real estate broker will have access to one or more "multi-list" capabilities. Moreover, although he or she probably will not be an attorney, a professional real estate broker is likely to be knowledgeable concerning real estate title and closing document issues.

If the seller desires to engage a real estate professional, he should check with other people in the project to obtain the names of brokers who have been successful in selling condominiums at the project, who have established a rapport with the board of directors or its management company, and who otherwise understand the obligations of the real estate broker and the seller concerning condominium documents and the state statutes regarding the sale of a condominium unit. He should be careful not to pick a real estate broker who lacks knowledge of condominiums, since, if he does so, he may sell the condominium but buy a lawsuit from his purchaser or condominium association, based upon his failure to comply with the law or condominium documents.

The seller does not want a real estate person who will make false or misleading statements to the purchaser concerning condominium living or what the purchaser can do at that condominium. Doing so will cause problems for both the real estate broker and seller.

The seller, in his listing agreement with the broker, should have a provision that the broker has no authority to make representations concerning the condition and nature of the premises except as expressly set forth in the Listing Agreement or the Purchase Agreement. By doing so, the seller helps to insulate himself from potential liability for misrepresentations by the broker in excess of his authority.

Regardless of whether the seller engages a real estate broker, the seller should consider employing an attorney to advise him concerning his responsibilities, as seller, to the purchaser and condominium association. A developing body of statutory and case law holds that sellers and/or their sales representatives must disclose all known or readily determinable facts which the purchaser would consider material to his decision to purchase, including, without limitation, facts concerning defects and deficiencies in the condominium unit. It is likely that the required disclosures apply both to the unit being sold (that is, typically, the cubicle of space the seller owns outright) and, if known, to the nature and condition of the "common elements."

The seller may wish to confirm with the board of directors the status of any assessments that are due and owing on his unit, and to determine whether the board intends to levy any special assessments in the near future. If a special assessment has been levied and is payable in installments, the seller should advise his attorney of that fact so arrangements for the proration of that assessment may be made in the purchase agreement.

Once the seller has decided whether he wishes to hire a professional real estate broker and/or has engaged a qualified attorney, he should notify the condominium association, if required by the condominium documents, of his intent to sell the unit. There may be another advantage to doing so, since many associations maintain a list of prospective purchasers or an in-house real estate person to help co-owners sell units. The seller also should verify that the association has complied with FNMA-FHLMC and other secondary mortgage lender requirements that will be important to a purchaser when he seeks financing. (If the association has not obtained FNMA or FHLMC approval, for example, the association may be able to do so by merely providing information to the secondary mortgage market representative.)

Finally, the seller should indicate in the purchase agreement that the assessments of the association may increase substantially and that the seller has no direct control over the nature and extent of the assessment being levied by the condominium association. Of course, if the seller is presently on the board of directors, then an additional disclaimer should be included regarding his activities as a director of the association, that is, to the effect that he assumes no responsibilities regarding the operation of the association to the purchaser.

"AS IS, WHERE IS"

If there are any defects or deficiencies in his unit that the seller knows, or suspects, exist, he should get an inspection report and provide it to a prospective purchaser, together with an adequate disclaimer in bold print that the purchaser is buying the condominium unit in an "as is" condition, without express or implied warranties, guaranties or representations of any type. The purchaser should be encouraged to obtain his own inspection report, if necessary, and the purchase agreement should reflect that advice.

Similarly, the seller should clearly indicate that the common elements of the condominium project are not guaranteed in any way, and that the purchaser is obligated to and acknowledges that he has inspected (or has had adequate opportunity to make his own investigation of) the condition of the common elements, and that he is buying the same as part of his unit on an "as is, where is" basis, without express or implied warranties, guaranties or representations of any type as to their condition, composition or nature.

If the association does allow the placement of a "for sale" sign in a window or elsewhere in his unit, the realtor or the seller may choose to use that opportunity. A word to the wise. If signs are not allowed and your lawyer advises you, based on the facts that you have provided him, that the prohibition against "for sale" signs is enforceable, you should follow the dictates of the condominium documents and not have the sign posted in your condominium.

Moreover, if a purchaser is found, you should comply with any "right of first refusal" that the condominium documents provide to the association. Many condominium projects, particularly the older ones, contain a "right of first refusal" that gives the association the right to buy your unit on the same terms and conditions as that of a bona fide prospective purchaser.

"Rights of first refusal" are rarely exercised and are rarely found in the condominium documents of newer condominiums, particularly because VA and other secondary mortgage lenders prohibit such provisions because of their susceptibility to abuse. Rights of first refusal have always been subject to the claim that their threatened exercise is merely a subterfuge for the board of directors to discriminate on the basis of race, color, creed, religion, national origin, etc. They cannot lawfully be used for discriminatory purposes.

Nevertheless, the right of first refusal has been upheld by courts if the association follows criteria that do not relate to legally prohibited classifications but, instead, are based upon sound economic principles. For example, while it would be improper for an association to exercise its right of first refusal with the intention to keep an Asian couple from buying a unit in the condominium, it would be reasonable for that association to exclude a person with a notoriously bad credit rating.

In many states, the condominium documents may contain reasonable restrictions on the sale and leasing of units. Not infrequently, these restrictions limit the number of units that may be leased in order to comply with requirements of the secondary mortgage market. More frequently, the seller must provide the condominium association with the details of sale. Such details may include the name of the purchaser, the terms and conditions of purchase, the name of the mortgage company and a certification that the purchaser has received a complete set of the condominium documents and acknowledges his willingness and obligation to comply with them. The association may have recourse against the seller if he fails to comply with this covenant.

It is in the seller's best interest to cooperate with the condominium association to avoid problems that may arise if the association has rights that were not exercised because it did not have actual knowledge of the sale. Moreover, the seller will wish to avoid causing problems for the purchaser with the association since the purchaser will, no doubt, seek recourse against the seller for his failure to comply with the obligations of the condominium documents. Of course, the purchaser should not be naive as to the seller's obligations and may wish to be assured that the seller has complied with all obligations of the condominium documents and relevant state statutes regarding the sale of the unit.

Assuming that the prerequisites of the condominium documents have been satisfied by the giving of notice to the condominium association, and that the sale is to be consummated, the seller should take the same precautions concerning the purchase agreement as he would in the sale of any other type of residential or commercial property. The purchase agreement should be in writing, spelling out, among other things, the basis by which all prorations of taxes, condominium assessments, both regular and special, and any reserve or working capital deposits will be made. Perhaps the most common mistake made by the seller or purchaser of residential real estate of any kind is the assumption that the purchase agreement is a formality, and that legal advice is not needed until the transaction is closed (if then). Nothing could be further from the truth. Too often, the attorney's hands are tied by the time he is first consulted!

THE REAL ESTATE CLOSING

Once a purchase agreement has been drafted and reviewed by

legal counsel (preferably, before it becomes binding), the seller should assist his real estate broker and/or attorney to obtain and provide to the purchaser the information necessary to satisfy any conditions to the purchase agreement becoming binding. For instance, it will be necessary to provide to the purchaser a complete set of the condominium documents—including any updates and/or amendments—together with the current rules and regulations of the condominium association, if any. Doing this in a timely fashion will also avoid any questions later as to whether the purchaser had actual notice of his obligations as a co-owner under the condominium documents.

If the seller has previously obtained permission from the association to make modifications, either permanent or temporary, to the common elements, those approvals should be disclosed to the purchaser prior to the execution of a purchase agreement (particularly if the approval is temporary). And if the modifications were only temporary, the seller should prepare to remove the modification. (The prudent condominium association, if it allowed modifications but imposed liability on the seller for continual maintenance, repair or replacement responsibility for the modifications, will have had an agreement prepared, executed and recorded in the land title records so that any new purchaser is on constructive notice of those responsibilities.)

If the seller has not already done so, the seller also will have to provide at this time whatever information he is required by state statutory or common law to provide to his purchaser concerning his knowledge of defects or deficiencies in the condominium unit. If the condominium unit was constructed prior to 1978, federal law also will require the disclosure of information concerning the presence, or absence, of lead paint. If the unit is being rented, the seller should provide the purchaser with a copy of the lease, assuming that he has not already done so.

Having provided the purchaser with the condominium documents and other necessary information, the seller should prepare for the closing of the unit with his real estate agent and/or attorney. Part of the obligation of the seller is to insure that the assessments have been paid up to date. The purchaser should protect his interests by requesting a letter from the condominium association indicating how much, if any, is owed to the condominium association for assessments. In Michigan, for example, this request must be made at least five (5) days before closing. The seller, if he is living in the unit, should prepare to move and should make sure he is leaving all items he is obligated by the purchase agreement to leave in the unit.

If the seller is leasing the unit and the purchaser intends to occupy the unit at closing, or shortly thereafter, the seller and purchaser should ensure that there will not be a problem in obtaining possession of the premises from the tenant(s). The seller should have looked at the lease arrangement to determine what rights he has against the tenant. Unless the lease will be assumed by the purchaser, he should make arrangements with the tenant to vacate the premises by a date certain. The seller should be careful, however, that he has left enough time to obtain possession of the premises from his tenant before the closing of the unit or the time when he must surrender possession to the purchaser.

The horror story that sometimes manifests itself is the tenant of the seller who refuses to vacate the premises on time. (The same situation may arise when the seller is unable to move into his new residence and, consequently refuses to leave the old.) The purchaser then sues the seller for breach of contract because the seller has failed to deliver possession on the date promised. Obviously, a purchaser will wish to have a penalty clause in the purchase agreement that provides adequate compensation if the purchaser is not given possession on the date promised, whether or not the seller is in possession of the premises. Conversely, the seller will try to negotiate adequate flexibility in the date of possession to ensure that he can deliver possession to the purchaser when he is required to do so. The seller should attempt to resist penalty clauses concerning the date of possession if he can negotiate around it.

By the date of closing, the prudent seller should have reviewed the closing documents with his attorney and real estate person to ensure that they are in order. In the case of a condominium, it is absolutely imperative that the correct unit description and appurtenances, such as the garage or carport if separately delineated, are conveyed by the warranty deed of conveyance. The seller should be obligated, under most circumstances, to provide a title insurance policy in the amount of the purchase price to the purchaser. The seller should ensure, and a competent title company will require, that the seller provide an affidavit that he has paid off all contractors and suppliers who have performed work on the premises within a certain period before the date of closing to ensure that there are not, and will not, be any liens later recorded against the unit.

Again, it is important that the seller "take care of business" before closing to provide time to cure any problems which may be identified. The seller should invite the purchaser to inspect the unit shortly before closing, and should request that he sign an acknowledgment that the condition of the unit at closing is satisfactory and is in accordance with the purchase agreement, that is, the same as it was when the purchaser first examined the unit before the purchase agreement was signed.

The prudent seller will make available to the purchaser at closing the necessary keys and information concerning the operation of various utilities, etc., serving the condominium unit, and should otherwise be as cooperative as possible. The seller should notify the condominium association that the closing has taken place and vacate the premises in a timely manner.

If all the above items are accomplished, the sale of a unit

should be smooth and uneventful. The co-owner will have sold his condominium unit to a purchaser who is knowledgeable about his responsibilities as a purchaser of the condominium, and the condominium association will be satisfied that the seller has complied with his obligations under the condominium documents and has made reasonable efforts to apprise the purchaser of his obligations. The real estate broker will have created good will with the association because he followed the dictates of the condominium documents and policies of the association.

Many of my recommendations regarding the sale of a condominium hold true for the sale of any type of residential housing. What makes the sale of a condominium unit complex and unique is the imposition of the rights of the condominium association and the condominium documents upon the sales transaction. With the assistance of prudent, competent counsel and a knowledgeable real estate person, the sale of a condominium unit can be a non-event. The purchase price obtained by the seller will relate directly, in most instances, to the manner in which the unit has been maintained and the viability of the project and condominium association as a whole. It is fair to say that a well-run project and condominium association enhances the marketability of all condominium units. It is also fair to say that the seller who adheres to my recommendations will, more than likely, avoid future problems arising from the sale of his condominium unit.

TAX RAMIFICATIONS

You should have considered the tax ramifications of selling your condominium unit before you signed a purchase agreement. Regardless, having successfully unloaded your unit without legal liabilities and entanglements, the Internal Revenue Service will now give you no choice but to do so.

Although this book is not intended as a tax treatise on the ramifications of real estate disposition, it is important to highlight some of the salient sections that may interest the average lay person considering buying or selling a condominium. Although I do not profess to have any particular expertise in tax matters, and this book is not designed to be a substitute for sound advice from a tax attorney or accountant, it may be helpful for you to understand some of the general tenets applicable to the transfer of real estate.

The rules governing the sale of one's principal residence are now contained in Section 121 of the Internal Revenue Code and summarized in IRS Publication 523. In general, a taxpayer may exclude from gross income up to $250,000 in capital gain ($500,000 in the case of a married taxpayer filing jointly, assuming that both husband and wife qualify) realized from the sale of his "main home" if **both** the "ownership" and "use" tests also are satisfied. (Note that this is an exclusion, not merely a deferral, of capital gain.) There are no longer any limitations upon the number of times that the exclusion may be utilized, assuming that the main home, ownership and use tests are in each case met, but the taxpayer must not have excluded gain from the sale of another home within the two (2) year period preceding the current sale.

Publication 523 states that a main home may be a house, houseboat, mobile home, cooperative apartment or condominium. Generally, your main home is the one you live in most of the time. Consequently, it is the position of the Internal Revenue Service that a person whose main home is a property he rents will not qualify for the exclusion. If you have more than one home, you can only exclude gain from the sale of your main home. The usual capital gain rules will apply to the sale of the other home(s) unless they will qualify as property held for business or investment purposes.

The ownership test requires that the taxpayer have owned the home for at least two (2) years during the five (5) year period ending on the date of sale. The use test requires that the taxpayer has lived in the home as his or her main home for at least two (2) years during the same five (5) year period. Short absences, such as for a summer vacation, count as periods of use, but longer absences, such as a one (1) year sabbatical, do not.

The reader should note that the ownership and use periods need not be concurrent, so a taxpayer who rents and lives in the home during, say, years one and two of the five-year period, and then purchases and rents the property for the remainder of the period, might qualify to exclude the gain. Finally, proposed IRS regulations will recognize a partial exclusion when the taxpayer fails to satisfy either the ownership or use test due to "unforeseen circumstances," which are defined to include, among others, death, divorce or legal separation, multiple births or a change in employment that requires relocation.

Although capital gain from the sale of one's main home may now be excluded up to the amount of the limitations described above, the rules remain complex, particularly if the taxpayer has multiple homes or the main home has been used for both residential and business or investment purposes during the five (5) year period preceding sale. Consequently, I recommend that a tax professional be consulted.

Now, you good troopers are about to focus on Section 1031, which permits the tax-free exchange of "like-kind" property held for an investment purpose, or for use in a trade or business, for those of you who are treating your condominium as an investment or as business property. Exchanges of investment and business property have never achieved wide popularity in much of the nation. This is partly because setting up a successful exchange often takes much more patience and homework than arranging a straight purchase and sale of property. Most brokers and investors simply do not understand the potentials of the exchange, or are frightened off by the intricate footwork that sometimes must take place to comply with the strict requirements imposed by the Internal Revenue Code.

The key advantage of the Section 1031 tax-free exchange is that the gain which otherwise would be realized need not be recognized at that time (i.e., tax may not be required to be paid on the gain at the time of sale), except that gain (but not a loss) must be recognized to the extent that money or property which is not like-kind property is received. With that exception, the tax is postponed until a reachable tax disposition occurs on the newly-received property. The advantage of this tax postponement is obvious. A series of "exchanges" may permit the deferral of tax recognition indefinitely, and if the property ends up in the estate of the exchanger with a stepped-up basis, tax may be avoided permanently.

Beside the tax advantages, an exchange (whether tax-free or not) can be used as a financing tool, since it permits the substitution of real estate for cash. The investor can reinvest his full capital in new properties without diminution due to tax payments. Uncle Sam, in effect, extends an interest-free loan to the investor, who may leverage his investment to a degree beyond that which may be obtained through mortgage financing.

With the described exception, Section 1031 (a) of the Internal Revenue Code provides that no gain or loss on an exchange of real estate is recognized on property held for productive use in a trade or business, or held for investment, if exchanged solely for property of a like kind which is to be held for productive use in a trade or business, or held as an investment.

Note that the exchange qualifies for tax-free treatment as long as each of the properties involved in the exchange is either property held for productive use in a trade or business **or** is property held for investment. Thus, property held for productive use in a trade or business may be exchanged for property held for investment. Similarly, property held for investment may be exchanged for property held for productive use in a trade or business. For the real estate investor, the major exception covers "stock in trade" or other property held "primarily for resale." This exclusion is intended to bar "dealers" in real estate (as distinguished from investors and businessmen) from obtaining the benefits of tax-free exchanges. There are companies that now specialize in tax-free exchange arrangements. But consult with your tax advisor first.

PART II The Operation of a
Condominium Association

Now that you know how to select, buy and sell a condo, it's time
to consider how condominium associations are supposed to operate—and how they actually *do* operate.

CHAPTER 7 | Cast of Characters
The Board of Directors

I have suggested that there are problems associated with the operation of the condominium association. I have offered suggestions concerning the prospective purchaser's investigation of a condominium and the co-owner's need to continually monitor the affairs of the condominium association. There is an old axiom (at least, I have asserted it for more than 30 years) that a condominium association is as good as its members, but especially its directors.

The role of a condominium board is not dissimilar from the role of the board of any other corporation. It should be clear to the enlightened reader (which you must be, since you haven't burned this book ... so far) that the role the board plays is, in short, the most important factor determining the success of community association operations. The board can, literally, make or break a condominium association. If the board is ineffectual, unreasonably dictatorial, myopic, vindictive, ignorant, inflexible, naive, unenlightened, self-serving and/or unwilling or unable to adhere to the condominium documents and general corporate law, the association is in for a heap of trouble!

What is the role of the board? The board administers the affairs of the project in accordance with state law and the condominium documents. It maintains, repairs and replaces the common elements for which the association is assigned responsibility under the condominium documents.

The role of the board includes long-range planning of the financial and physical condition of the condominium. That means establishing procedures for maintaining the condominium, collecting assessments, enforcing condominium restrictions, rules and regulations, and the like. The board also sets procedures for the holding of annual and special meetings of the association and for the letting of necessary contracts on behalf of the association, and seeks to ensure that the reasonable needs and concerns of the co-owners regarding the administration of the condominium project are met.

The board of directors is the administrator of the condominium association. It establishes policies regarding the functioning of the association within the jurisdictional limits set by state law and the condominium documents.

WHAT MAKES A GOOD BOARD?

If the board is so large and unwieldy that the association's business cannot be conducted in an efficient manner, that alone may detract from the successful operation of the condominium association. For example, nine directors for a 45-unit complex is too many, even though it is commonly said that there is safety in numbers. Not so in condominiums ... except, perhaps, in the swimming pool!

In order for a board of directors to be effective, it must intelligently carry out its responsibilities. That may require that the board employ a management firm and other consultants to help the board discharge its responsibilities. What is important to remember is that the board has the obligation, in most instances, to pick the management company, lawyer, architect or engineer, insurance agent and other contractors or consultants that the board needs to help it discharge its responsibilities. If the board members do not understand the condominium documents, and do not seek legal counsel or other consultants to help them understand and interpret the condominium documents, they cannot properly discharge their responsibilities. In fact, in too many instances, boards do not discharge all of their responsibilities.

The single greatest problem that I have observed in the operation of condominium associations over the years is the almost universal unwillingness of boards of directors to spend money. Any honest, service-related person associated with community associations will concur. For some reason, the directors believe that their primary responsibility is to save money, sometimes at whatever cost!

The board of directors needs to establish a feasible maintenance program for the association. Not that it must paint everyone's unit every year. However, the board must properly maintain and repair those common elements of the condominium for which the association has legal responsibility. What is reasonable maintenance and repair is within the discretion of the board. If the board is extraordinarily frugal and refuses to make necessary repairs to the common areas, disenchanted co-owners may have redress against the board for the association's failure to maintain those areas, regardless of the economic condition of the association.

A board that is unwilling to spend the money necessary in order to properly maintain and administer the condominium is a board that is not doing its job. Admittedly, how much to spend on maintenance may be a matter of judgment on the part of each board. However, some boards have hidden behind the thinly masked veil of "discretion" in repair priorities to justify their unwillingness, or inability, to properly meet the needs of association members.

Certainly, the standard of care in an FHA-subsidized condominium project will differ from that in a project with units priced in excess of $300,000. On the other hand, I have observed condominiums with units ranging in price between $50,000 and $75,000 that were better maintained by the association than projects whose units cost in excess of $300,000. Usually, this has been the result of the board of the lesser-priced condominium having adopted a more aggressive maintenance policy than the more expensive project.

The role of the board includes assuring that the decisions of the board are uniform, consistent, enforced vigorously and with dispatch. The board should enforce prohibitions within the condominium documents concerning exterior modifications, dogs running loose on the common elements, parking in areas not designated for such, unreasonable activities by co-owners that are a disturbance to neighbors, and the like.

Unfortunately, in almost every condominium, the board, at some time or another, has made exceptions to the dictates of the bylaws, rules and regulations of the condominium. For example, not unexpectedly, one finds that directors have friends in the condominium (at least initially) and, therefore, they are sometimes unwilling to enforce bylaw restrictions or the rules and regulations against their friends.

SEEKING OUTSIDE HELP

On multiple occasions, I have experienced painful situations where name-calling, and even physical assault, has occurred among board members and/or members of the association enraged about the operation of the association. Verbal fights over the selection of a management company (or whether to obtain professional management), over the selection of a lawyer or snow removal contractor, or whether the developer should be sued, or whether speed bumps should be installed, are but a few examples of issues that have opened schisms within boards and/or between members of the association.

Many vendors and professionals are reluctant, or unwilling, to deal with community associations. The perception is that the community association board member may lack a clear understanding of the proper operation of the association or of sound business principles, or that his actions may be arbitrary, whimsical, capricious or unprofessional, or that he is likely to engage in the intimidation or harassment of co-owners or other board members.

The concern is that such conduct, and the perception of vendors and professionals, may deprive community associations of competent and reasonable choices for management firms, service firms, accountants, lawyers and other consultants. How often have you heard a service-related person complain about how difficult it is to deal with a community association board?

That is not to say that all, or even most, boards of directors fall within this mold. It just seems to those of us who have dealt with condominium associations that such personalities surface at inopportune times.

ESTABLISHING SUBCOMMITTEES

The role of the board includes the obligation to establish a committee structure, appoint officers and solicit the help of association members to assist the board in establishing and implementing policies and directives. While the board should rely on outside persons (who have no proprietary interest in the condominium project) to assist the board with matters of law, accounting, insurance and management, the board should recruit association members to serve on committees to help discharge the responsibilities of the board.

Boards commonly appoint, among others, an architectural control committee, a budget and finance committee, a buildings and grounds keeping committee, a bylaws committee, a social committee, a welcoming committee and a newsletter committee. Many times, these committees are composed of people who have run unsuccessfully for the board of directors, who have served on the board in the past, or who have been solicited by the board to prepare for ascendancy to a directorship.

Unfortunately, most boards of directors fail to organize a viable committee structure. An association that lacks a viable committee structure is unlikely to enjoy broad-based co-owner participation or an effective board succession. Worse yet, apathy, perhaps the greatest enemy of the successful community association, may develop.

Condominiums are particularly susceptible to apathy because the carefree living myth has been perpetuated by developers, sales agents and the media. Most people who buy a condominium do so to disengage themselves from the operation and maintenance of their home.

The question of combating apathy in the condo association could likely warrant a chapter of its own. Suffice it to say that the role of the board includes eliciting support from association members regarding the activities and programs of the board, and one of the best ways to accomplish this is through a committee structure.

One of the best ways to get co-owners to participate in the association is to persuade them that it is in their own best interest to help the association function effectively. One way to sell them on that concept is to have an annual meeting with social activities attendant to it.

A condominium association that our firm represents frequently has its annual meetings at a lounge. Libations are available to the members before, during and after the meeting. While there were instances of excess, in most instances, this technique has created an atmosphere in which the co-owners feel more comfortable in attending and participating in the meeting.

Conversely, scare tactics also may elicit participation by the members. Frequently, when the association is engaged in litigation with the developer, for example, the board can convince members to list defects and deficiencies, serve on committees to solicit information necessary to assist the attorney and make the co-owners recognize that their investment in the condo is at stake. In order to solicit additional support and help, many self-managed condominiums threaten association members with the substantial additional cost that will result if a professional management company is retained.

Many associations simply cannot get good people to run for the board or, perhaps, the "good" people are not encouraged to run for the board. There also may be a situation where the directors wish to perpetuate their power and overtly, or covertly, discourage the participation of other members.

In soliciting members of the association, the nominating committee should "hammer home" the fact that the quality of life in the condominium will reflect the quality of the board and its committee structure. This theme should be continuously promoted in newsletters, circulars, meetings of the association and the like to crystallize to the co-owner that his participation in the association is necessary (assuming that he is not a certifiable lunatic).

But will they then do something constructive? Since the role of the director requires a substantial amount of time, energy, and expertise, and since condominium association directors usually are not compensated, this "good" volunteer director many times burns out, becomes disgusted or acquiesces to the whims of the "crazies."

GETTING INVOLVED

Ideally, the board of directors will consist of people who are willing to dedicate their time and energies to running the business of the condominium association in a professional and businesslike manner. Ideally, again, the board will be composed of fair-minded individuals who understand the director's role, will operate in good faith, will avoid conflicts of interest and self-dealing, and will recognize that the expenditure of condominium association funds may be necessary for the proper administration of the project and the proper maintenance and repair of the common elements.

Unfortunately, the activities of the directors are frequently different in quality from that of a "for-profit" corporation. That is simply a problem with condominium living and operation under the present governing structure.

Volunteer board members are, by definition, uncompensated, are not trained for their positions, are many times unwilling to accept the position, are, too often, unable to adapt to the requirements of the position and are again, too often elected to the position for the wrong reasons. Simply put, directors and officers frequently lack the psychological, economic, educational, and business acumen necessary to balance the political, economic, legal and social realities of condominium living within the framework of the community association.

Notwithstanding the "crazies," the smart co-owner will engage in some activity to promote the successful operation of the association, if for no other reason than to monitor the affairs of the association and its board to protect his investment and peace of mind. The perceptive co-owner will investigate the infrastructure of the condominium association board and assess whether its members fit any of the personality categories set forth in this book. This monitoring process should be ongoing, particularly if there are changes in the composition of the board.

JUDGING THE ASSOCIATION BY THE BOARD

A new co-owner should investigate the "cast of characters" on the board of directors, since the board will have a direct and profound impact, for better or for worse, upon the co-owner's experience with life in the condominium. Prospective purchasers also should try to gauge the directors' economic and educational backgrounds. The co-owner should arrange, if possible, to meet one or more of them personally to get a sense of what he has gotten into at the condominium. The co-owner also should consider whether he wishes to participate in its governing structure.

As frightening as it may seem, the directors of condo associations wield tremendous power, similar, albeit on a lesser scale, to their counterparts in government. Typically, condo associations are vested with extraordinary power to regulate the activities of the co-owners. For this reason, the co-owner must seriously consider whether direct input to the board of directors is necessary in order to protect his investment—and perhaps his sanity.

The types of personalities one may discover on his board of directors deserve a psychological evaluation, albeit amateurish. If these descriptions of typical community association directors concern you (as they should), take note before it is too late!

Remembering that condominium associations and their directors are microcosms of society, there will be a director or two who is extremely aggressive and claims, or perhaps usurps, the role of leader in the condominium. This outspoken person (I will call him a "dictator") tends overtly, or covertly, to seize control of the board of directors. The dictator may believe that he or she is "destined" to serve on the board for years to come. This person may be well-intentioned, but, at some psychological level, generally has a need to serve as a leader of the community, if for no other reason than that he has never exercised this type of responsibility in his life. Frequently, the dictator is unwilling to share his power with other directors.

While generalizations are not always valid, I have found that engineers (or their progeny) frequently assume positions of power on boards of directors, perhaps because of their training and need for precision. The archetype "engineer" director wants things done in his way, and only his way, and often wants to redo everything that has transpired before him, since it was not good enough.

You are less likely to find this type of individual in the "blue collar" condominium, where members are more likely to recognize their individual limitations, than in affluent condominiums. The "professional person" may seize the opportunity to exert his supposed knowledge and expertise over people who, though they may have greater expertise, don't wish to participate on the board of directors because of apathy, ignorance or lifestyle.

Of course, the dictator does not have to be an engineer. He could be a male who is constantly yelled at by his wife and finds that the board of directors offers an opportunity to assert himself. The dictator could be the housewife who has raised three kids, has never ventured into the business world and is now frustrated that she may not have lived up to her potential. Beware of an association that has this type of leader, as he or she is too often likely to emasculate all rational voices that are not as assertive or outspoken!

If the board harbors a dictator, and the dictator is able to cause the other directors to blindly follow his dictates or whims, be they altruistic or otherwise, the board is inevitably doomed to failure. On some occasions, the dictator is likely to lead the board astray or to impose his personal biases on the remainder of the members to the detriment of the association as a whole.

If the director-tyrant controls the association newsletter, he may be able to hoodwink the association members into thinking that his path is absolutely wise and just. However, the board that is run in this fashion, by this kind of individual, may ultimately find itself sued.

On the other hand, the dictator can make a legitimate contribution to the board if, although assertive, he is consensus-oriented, rather than dictatorial. It is important to have someone on the board who can bring diverse thoughts and attitudes together to reach some sense of order in the form of a consensus. Lack of continuity is a huge problem in condominium governance; the dictator who has been on the board for 10 years may contribute continuity and a morbid, if not necessarily historically accurate, perspective (assuming that he is willing to share it with the other directors).

You may also find on the board the personality type that I will describe as the "schoolteacher." The schoolteacher may have no other reason for serving on the board than a messianic zeal to teach, albeit extracurricularly! Unfortunately, the schoolteacher may lack business acumen and, perhaps, common sense, and also may be easily intimidated to follow the dictates of the dictator. Although the schoolteacher is reasonably intelligent, he or she is passive and does not understand why the condo association is there to begin with. Generally, she will oppose any suggestion that the board should spend money to obtain the professional assistance of lawyers or accountants.

You may wonder at the schoolteacher's myopic view of the world. She views the world as a great "lesson plan." She may indulge in professional hyperbole when she is rattled or in order to impress other members of the board!

You may find on your board of directors the "construction worker" personality. He ran for the board of directors because his wife told him to do so. He jumped at the chance because he was looking for a way to get out of the house in the evening!

The construction worker director is generally worthless and follows the lead of others, contributing little of import. This director can be easily manipulated by the dictator, and even by the schoolteacher, to make decisions that do not serve the best interests of the association. He is likely to volunteer for the social committee, and his most thoughtful suggestion may be to organize an association bowling league!

In affluent condominiums, a "doctor" or two will serve on the board of directors. The doctor will want to run the association in his own image and has an inherent distrust of lawyers and other "lesser" professionals. He will, of course, not want to spend money. He will likely not understand why the condominium documents must be followed. Instead, consistent with his "Hippocratic Oath," he wishes to "do no harm."

In deference to Shakespeare, I cannot spare the "lawyers." (Shakespeare would, no doubt, write a trilogy about condos, co-ops and PUDs, were he alive.) On rare occasions, the lawyer may be a much-needed voice of reason. Too often, the lawyer will instead be a self-proclaimed expert in condominium law and operation who has little real experience in real estate law and, usually, less in the law of condominiums. Of course, that won't stop him from giving legal advice!

Finally, let's not forget the "successful entrepreneur." Believe it or not, a businessman can be a detriment to a condominium association. Even though the businessman may have made millions, he may be unable to appreciate that the condominium association cannot be operated like his country club, where the "boys" do as they like. Often, this type of director will be the most detrimental, since his success and, perhaps, wealth, will command respect from the other directors. He cares little for the condominium documents and discounts the advice of the association's attorney, accountant and management firm.

In the "blue collar" condominium project, the success of the board may depend upon the education of its directors. The members of the association may have little understanding of the manner in which a community association should function, so the board will soon learn that the members are easily persuaded by an assertive style. The directors of a blue-collar project are more likely to disavow the rules, or to look for shortcuts in the enforcement of the condominium documents, and they may even accept compensation for their activities when that is forbidden by the condominium documents!

In condominiums whose members are mostly retirees, the now-retired dictator will project stubbornness, or senility. The bottom line, as he sees it, is to spend no money because everyone is presumed to be on a fixed income. Beware of that kind of project as an investment or a place for your parents to live! The association will be unable to meet the reasonable needs of the condominium project and will soon become dysfunctional.

This is not to say that retirement communities are impractical, or that the presence of senior citizens on the board of directors suggests that the condominium will be a bad investment. Rather, I fear, the mentality of frugality that permeates the board of directors in these environs leaves little room for business sense or proper condominium operation.

On a senior citizen-dominated board, there may be less openness to new ideas and thoughts, and less likelihood that professional management and assistance will be obtained. Although the board of directors establishes policy, it must retain persons to carry out that policy, including management agents, snow removal contractors, lawyers, accountants and insurance agents. An unwillingness to do so breeds trouble.

The quality of the director will have a direct bearing on the success of the condominium association. It is not unreasonable, therefore, for an individual to evaluate each of the directors when buying a condominium or when deciding whether to participate in the affairs of the association. You may be able to make a difference in how your association operates, if for no other reason than your involvement on the board may prevent some "crazy" of the type described from assuming control of the board, to the detriment of all.

My law firm strongly recommends that clients take part in the activities of the association from their very first affiliation with the project, whether or not the association is controlled by the developer. As a whole, our clients tend to be more enlightened than many of the directors who take control of the association—and tend to make significant contributions to the association.

Remember that a well-run association can deteriorate overnight with the resignation of one or more directors or the election of one or more new directors. It should come as no major revelation that, because of the divisiveness that frequently permeates condominium boards, a change in the swing vote of one director may have a profound effect upon the decisions reached by the board of directors on crucial issues.

Abuses of board power are not uncommon in this situation. Board members have literally been thrown off the board, without authority or justification. More typically, the "good" directors simply become disgusted with the malcontent directors who impose their crazed and senseless will on the other directors.

Proxy battles for control of the association also are relatively common. Directors disagree concerning the operation of the association, with the result that the minority "takes its case" to association members, or to the municipality. Through perseverance and the deterioration or stagnation of the condominium, even the most unenlightened co-owners may realize the board must be changed.

THE IDEAL DIRECTOR

Ideally, the board should be composed of directors who have a sense of their responsibility, who understand the condominium documents, who understand the condominium association is a business and that it should be run as such. They should understand that in running that business, the association needs those persons and/or consultants necessary to assist the board in operating this strange beast called the condominium association.

Unfortunately, most of the time, directors do not have that sense, and they may really believe that they are entrusted with the obligation to assure that the association spends as little money as possible, whatever the cost. They are intimidated by co-owners, are unwilling to make decisions, are unwilling to stand up at board meetings to express their views and, too often, reach, what I tell my condominium law students, is a "consensus of ignorance." Frequently, this consensus of ignorance involves an issue that requires particular expertise or knowledge, generally in the engineering or legal vein. In order to save money, the directors instead combine their "life experiences." They then reach a "common sense" consensus, which, many times, is dead wrong.

Beware of the condo board that acts this way! This will result in nothing but adverse legal and financial consequences to the condo association. If you're on such a board, remind the other directors of their fiduciary responsibility and duty to avoid conflicts of interest and self-dealing, all of which may lead to legal liability to the members.

In a nutshell, the composition of the board is crucial in evaluating the potential success of the condo association. Do your own psychological evaluation of the directors and the co-owners living in the condominium before you buy. If you're stuck in a situation with a director who is a "dictator" or "schoolteacher" type, see what you can do to build your own consensus on the board or through the association. Recognize that the operation of the association is a political affair, and that the dynamics that make a successful campaign for public office may well be applicable to condominium living. A successful director must be a sociologist, a psychologist, a lawyer, an astute businessman, an economist, a financial planner, and a consummate leader and teacher, all combined into one. If the directors collectively lack these attributes, watch out!

By the way, lunatic directors should be placed in that area of the condominium designated for off-road vehicles and the like. If you don't believe what I have preached in this chapter, attend a directors meeting or talk with a director or owner who has had to deal with a "loony" on the board of directors!

So, you want to live in a condo ... huh?

CHAPTER **8** The Man with the Plan
The Developer and Transition to
Condo Association Control

The role of the developer will now be considered in the context of the developer's control of the board of directors of the condominium association during the initial stages of operation of the condominium, which may be a period of years. The developer, if he, or his designee, serves as a board member at the same time he is developing the condominium project, must be cognizant of his responsibilities to the non-developer co-owners.

The developer must be multi-faceted. He must deal with the trades to get the condominium buildings completed. He must be a politician when dealing with the small percentage of determined malcontents who will be unhappy no matter what he does. He must be an economist when running the affairs of the association and establishing an adequate and realistic budget so that the co-owners will find that the assessment advertised to them by the developer is both realistic and pragmatic. And he must be a sociologist, able to determine if the restrictions to be imposed on the association members are both enforceable and manageable.

Conceptually, the role of the developer is to develop the condominium project, that is, construct or convert the condominium units for occupancy and prepare the members of the condominium association to take control of the project and run the condominium association. If the developer has done a good job of constructing or converting the units, has adequately funded the association, has a procedure by which the board of directors can be turned over to the co-owners in a smooth and efficient fashion, has prepared an operational procedure, perhaps including a manual of operations and a book of resolutions concerning bylaw enforcement, collection and other matters, then the developer will have fulfilled his role and will probably not get sued by the association.

Unfortunately, many developers do not build condominiums properly, that is, they fail to comply with minimum building code requirements or workmanship standards, or they fail to convert the condominium so the project is habitable, or cosmetically pleasing, resulting in serious problems for the association members. The developer may not properly fund the association, or may not establish or contribute to adequate reserves for the major repair and replacement of the common elements. Too often, developers fail to cause the association board of directors, while under their control, to enforce the condominium documents, thereby allowing modifications or changes that not only don't conform to the condominium documents prepared by the developer but are outside the authority of the board of directors to approve. A typical example might be the developer-controlled board that allows a co-owner (purchaser) to extend his or her deck onto the common elements, thereby causing an expropriation of the common elements by that co-owner without the consent of all necessary co-owners.

As previously stated, the directors of the association, be they designees of the developer or non-developer co-owners, assume legal and fiduciary responsibilities to the association and its members based on the condominium documents, common law and statutory law. The developer's failure to build the condominium properly, or to cause the association board of directors, while under the developer's control, to operate in the best interest of the non-developer co-owners, will, at best, be construed as a breach of the developer's fiduciary obligation. Consequently, the developer must totally understand his role as director of the association and the liability that he potentially incurs.

This inherent conflict of interest is a troublesome problem for the developer. If he is smart, he will appoint designees to the association board who are not directly related to him. That is, neither he nor any member of his family should be appointed; instead, he should appoint persons who are associated with him who will not be attractive litigation targets, usually because they have a minimal net worth. He should attempt, if possible, to get insurance for his designated directors while they serve on the board of directors.

The developer should assume a leadership role in this instance. The developer should not be shortsighted, thinking that his only task is to sell and market condos and then get out. Instead, the developer should establish, through properly drafted condominium documents, a vehicle that will work both now and in the future and can be adapted to the changing needs of the association and its members. The role of the developer requires that he promote the ability of the association members to take control of the association. A smart developer will establish operational procedures for dealing with common problems, such as collecting delinquent assessments, enforcing bylaw violations and dealing with warranty complaints. The developer should not ignore the needs of the association while he is in control or, for that matter, thereafter. The developer should establish a bond of trust and cooperation with the association members, which, in the long run, will stand the developer in good stead when developing future condo projects.

The developer has the opportunity to be a good citizen, both as the developer of the project and a member of the association. If the developer is not fulfilling this role, purchasers should avoid his project and he should be pursued legally by the condominium association.

Homeowners do not like starting lawsuits. They don't like to hire lawyers, and they will look for every excuse to resolve the dispute with the developer without resorting to court. It is only when they are pushed against the wall (a wall, built by the developer, which may have cracked) that condominium associations start lawsuits.

Developers sometimes get into trouble no matter what they do. But that's not normally the case. The enlightened and prudent developer can find condominium development a prosperous enterprise.

PREPARING FOR THE TURNOVER

While the condominium association is under the control of the developer, the co-owners will be virtually powerless to determine the destiny of the condominium project. Although most statutes and condominium documents provide for the formation of a "steering committee" or "advisory committee" of association members, many developers ignore this obligation. If they do comply with the obligation to form an advisory committee, they may appoint people they believe will serve the developer's interest in seeing that the condominium project is completed without interference from the co-owners.

Such developers are interested in selling units, not in preparing co-owners for the responsibilities of association operation.

The appointment of a token non-developer co-owner to a developer-controlled board may be a "no-win" situation for that director—and of no real benefit to the co-owners.

The result, when this occurs, is that condominium co-owners are handed control of the association without any idea as to what the operation of the association requires. When the co-owners do take control, they understandably are concerned whether they will thereby waive any rights that they may have to pursue the developer for construction deficiencies or other claims. It is imperative, therefore, that the developer adequately prepares the co-owners to take control of the association. If the developer is unwilling to do so, the co-owners should organize themselves and, if necessary, raise sufficient funds to retain legal counsel, an accountant and other professional advisers to assist the steering committee to prepare for the turnover meeting.

Beware of the developer who does not care about forming a steering committee. Be cautious of a steering committee not elected from association members.

I strongly recommend that you participate in the first co-owner controlled steering committee, which will serve as the precursor for future condominium association operations. You may find it prudent to have a social gathering of the co-owners at which you propose that a steering committee be organized, if the developer refuses to do so. If there are abuses by the developer respecting construction defects or inadequate financial contributions, bring these matters to the attention of both the developer and your co-owner neighbors and solicit their help to organize the steering committee.

This task may be your introduction to the frustrations in dealing with condominium co-owners. You will no doubt run across individuals who do not want to get involved for any reason, and who do not understand the need to organize before taking control of the association. They have naively accepted the notion that condominium living is "carefree living," rather than "careful living." They do not appreciate that the condominium fabric is tenuous at best. They do not understand that the success of the condominium project, after the developer has left, will directly relate to the success of its board's organization and operation. More than likely, they will be unwilling to pay for an attorney for the steering committee. Many community associations flounder, particularly at their initial stages, because the members cannot organize themselves.

The exception may be if they are experiencing a specific problem with the developer that they cannot resolve on their own, or if they have some other vested interest in pursuing the developer. Perhaps for less than altruistic reasons, then, the co-owners may contribute towards the organization of the association, while not understanding that it is in the interest of all members that the association begin on the "right foot." (The reader interested in more information on this topic may wish to consider the author's book, "Getting Started and Staying on the Right Track," 2nd Edition, which is referenced in the References section.) What can the enlightened purchaser/co-owner do at this point? He can try to alert association members who have already bought as to the obligations of the developer that are not being fulfilled, or to the commitment that they must make to organize the association. He must relate analogies that they can appreciate from their own business or professional experiences, which illustrate the dire consequences when an organization is not run properly.

If there is a rallying point around which all co-owners will gather, you will find that it is when the painting has not been completed, the roads are cracking or the basements are leaking. Such deficiencies can be used by the enlightened organizer to energize the other members of the association. On the other hand, when the developer's abuses are more subtle, such as when he has not made adequate financial contributions or has not organized the steering committee, or when the developer is "sweet talking" the homeowners into believing that everything will be OK, the organizer's task will be more formidable.

YOUR FUTURE IS IN THEIR HANDS

Unlike many other societal organizations, the condominium association must be run by its director-members, as opposed to outside participants who will assist the group. While the management company can serve as a buffer or aid to the successful operation of the condominium association, it is the board of directors that ultimately has the legal responsibility to decide how the association will function. The directors are rarely professional directors. Therefore, the quality of leadership and organizational skills of the persons operating the condominium after the developer leaves will, in many instances, be deficient, if for no other reason than that no one on the board has had any experience in operating a condominium association.

That is not to say that you will be unable to solicit volunteer co-owners to serve on the steering committee or the first board of directors. There are always those who are willing to participate in the operation of any organization. However, just because someone has served on another board of directors, or on a homeowners association, does not mean that he or she is a "good" condo board prospect. To the contrary. The process by which this person was appointed or elected to the previous board may have been just as inept, arbitrary or disorganized as is the process with which you are involved. There is no substitute for experience and there is no substitute for education.

It is surprising, but true, that a person who is a skilled businessman or an educated schoolteacher may not become a good condo director. Similarly, the manager of apartment complexes or other types of commercial enterprises may prove to be a poor condo director.

What will make a person a good condo director is his understanding of the role of the director, his business acumen, his knowledge of the condominium documents and procedures, and his sociological, psychological, legal and financial awareness. There may, in fact, be persons in the condominium association who fit that bill. Hopefully, you will join forces with them to organize the condo in a proper fashion. You will, however, run across directors who do not have the best interests of the condominium in mind, who do not have any sense of duty to the association and/or who do not have any idea of their role. It will be through the catharsis of the condo board meeting that you will learn about these individuals and their idiosyncrasies.

THE LEARNING EXPERIENCE

There are well-intentioned people who have the intellectual and psychological abilities to be good directors and leaders but lack relevant education, experience and/or just a "pat on the back." How can these people develop their skills?

First, anyone serving on an advisory or steering committee or on the board of directors should clearly understand the condominium documents.

Second, such persons should understand the dynamics of group decision-making. There is usually a consensus, which may not be the composite total of the opinions of each of the individual directors. In essence, the board decision is a compromise. It is this process of compromise that sometimes leads to improper or inappropriate decisions by members of the board or steering committee.

Third, it is beneficial to get as much literature as possible about the proper operation of the condominium and the successful operation of the association. Various area universities teach classes in the operation of condominium associations and the potential liabilities of directors and officers. Books on condominium operation should be reviewed by prospective purchasers and condominium directors to help them in maintaining and operating the condominium properly.

In short, there is no substitute for education and understanding of the condominium concept. The board of directors or steering committee should hire an attorney to advise it who is well versed in condominium association operation. Suffice it to say that the steering committee chairman's son-in-law, who just happens to be an attorney, ought not to be the association's first pick. Nor should the association select the cheapest condo lawyer in town, or a management company pawn. Rather, the board or steering committee should pick an experienced and knowledgeable attorney who is recognized as an expert in condominium law and can present to the board an effective outline for association operation.

AUDITS AT THE TURNOVER

Once a newly elected board of directors is in place and the developer has turned over all books, records, contracts, site drawings/plans and association materials requested by the board, the board should review the status of the condominium project. Optimistically, the advisory/steering committee, which preceded the board, will have done some initial work, and some of the members of the advisory committee may continue to serve as directors of the association after turnover.

The board should first determine the form of management. The alternatives that are available are:

- Self management;

- An on-site manager or resident manager (sometimes called an administrator);

- A professional management company to assist it in managing the day-to-day affairs of the association;

- A management consultant to assist it in particular needs of the condominium association, such as establishing a long-range reserve for a replacement program or even dealing with the yearly budget for the association; or,

- A combination of the above.

What things, then, should the non-developer board of directors consider when it takes over control of the association? There are four "audits" that ought to be undertaken by the board of directors. These audits should be made after the association board has been provided by its attorney with a checklist of items that should be considered before the developer is released of its legal responsibilities to the association. The developer and condo member association should be prepared to deal with these audits!

THE FINANCIAL AUDIT

The first type of audit to be conducted is an audit of the condominium association's financial affairs. This is necessary since the developer has previously controlled the board of directors. The board should know exactly what the fiscal condition of the association is, and whether the developer:

- Has paid to the association all the assessments it was obligated to pay;

- Spent association money on items which should properly have been the responsibility of the developer;

- Collected the proper amount of assessments from the co-owners; and

- Contributed adequate amounts of money to establish a

reserve for replacements for major repairs in the condominium and any other mandated reserves.

Unfortunately, a newly elected board may find that the association is under funded, or has a "loan" owed to the developer, because the developer has "low-balled" the assessments; that is, he has undercharged the amount of assessments necessary to adequately maintain the condominium association and to establish a reserve for replacements. This is particularly a problem with the conversion condominium project. At a minimum, to determine the exact financial condition of the association, the board must retain an experienced condominium accountant, preferably a CPA, to conduct a preliminary audit of the financial affairs of the association as of the time of turnover.

The developer should cooperate in turning over the books and records. Unfortunately, some developers comingle funds with those of their own companies and the books and records are in a state of disarray. If that is the case, the board should have even more concern about how the financial affairs of the association were conducted before turnover, and the services of a CPA experienced in condo audits will be essential. A certified audit will be an essential tool as the association attorney evaluates possible association claims against the developer for his financial mismanagement of the condo association.

THE LEGAL AUDIT

The second type of audit that the newly elected board should authorize when it takes control of the condominium association is the legal audit. The legal audit should be done by an experienced condominium attorney. He should review the condominium documents that were prepared by the developer to ensure that they are internally consistent, legally enforceable and in compliance with the applicable condominium statute.

He also should confirm that the documents take advantage of any recent changes to the condominium statute and general corporate law that would be helpful to the association. For example, several years ago in Michigan, a statute was passed providing nonprofit association directors, officers and volunteer committee persons protection from certain liabilities. The statutory protections can only become operative when a condominium association approves and files an amendment to its articles of incorporation. Other amendments to the condominium documents also may be necessary.

The legal audit should include a review of all contracts and other legal documents relating to the condominium association. The attorney for the association should review insurance contracts and determine whether the association has the type of insurance coverage that it is obligated to have under the condominium documents. For example, the attorney should ensure that the board has at least considered obtaining directors and officer's liability insurance, and in sufficient amounts. The legal audit should suggest a review of finances and the physical plant of the condominium project. Finally, the legal audit should recommend that the board of directors establish a book of resolutions concerning the collection of assessments, enforcement of the condominium documents, hearing procedures pertaining to fines, agreements regarding the modification of common elements, agreements concerning disabled persons and other matters that may be necessary to assist in the orderly operation of the association. A legal audit should be conducted periodically.

THE PHYSICAL AUDIT

The third type of audit to be performed at the time of turnover is the physical audit. The physical audit is a compilation of the defects and deficiencies in the common elements of the project for which the developer may be responsible. The developer has a legal responsibility to turn over the project in a proper and work-manlike condition, and if warranties have been extended expressly, implicitly or by operation of law, in a manner consistent with its terms.

The board of directors should pursue these potential claims against the developer, and also should establish a budget that includes adequate reserves for future repair and replacement of the physical plant of the project. It may be necessary for the board of directors to retain architects and/or engineers to help them to do so. Finally, the board should consider mailing a questionnaire, prepared under the auspices of the association attorney, requesting that the co-owners provide information concerning defects or deficiencies in the common areas that they have observed. The physical audit may be an ongoing process if there is ongoing construction by the developer.

The association board must consult with legal counsel, based on the results of the audit, to determine what recourse, if any, the association has to correct the defects and deficiencies in the physical plant of the condominium. The physical audit can also serve another important purpose: to evaluate the long-range useful life of the amenities of the project in order to properly fund reserves.

THE OPERATIONAL AUDIT

Finally, the board of directors should, with the advice and aid of counsel, engage in an operational audit of the project. The operational audit determines whether, in fact, the association is running smoothly and what part of its operation can be enhanced. What type of management form is best suited for the condominium association? Are there effective procedures for co-owner complaints, vehicle registration for parking, the compilation of voter designation forms, listings of the association members' names and addresses, and the like? Are board and association meetings properly and efficiently conducted?

In short, the operational audit is an attempt to ensure that adequate operating procedures are in place and that there are procedures to streamline and clarify those processes. The assistance of a professional management company or consultant is often helpful in ensuring proper operation of the condominium association.

So, too, are operational rules and resolutions for collections, bylaw enforcement, lease forms, modified agreements and formal service contracts. (See reference No. 5 on page 177.)

CHAPTER 9

Choosing Hired Help
The Condo Association Attorney, CPA and Insurance Agent

Among the most important considerations for the board of directors or officers of a condominium association is the advice and services of outside professionals to assist them in running the business of the condominium. While this may seem obvious to the lay reader, it is not a fact of life in the operation of all condominium associations.

Many times, the directors or officers of the association are individuals who have had no exposure to, or need for, an attorney, except perhaps in a divorce proceeding or in the defense of a drunk driving charge. On the other side of the spectrum is the corporate executive who has relied upon legal counsel his entire professional life and, since he's been successful in his business or occupation, is now "too smart" to need an attorney. These attitudes often permeate boards of directors, which results in a general reluctance to even interview an attorney.

Also, there is the belief among some that attorneys are expensive or will cause additional problems, rather than resolve them. While such generalizations are certainly not accurate, they occur with sufficient frequency that they cloud the thinking of many association directors and officers.

The fact is that the condominium association needs an attorney as much, and perhaps more, than any other business. Moreover, the co-owners need legal representation to protect their interests even before they take control of the association.

The need for legal representation begins when the developer establishes, or the co-owners organize, an advisory committee. The attorney chosen by the advisory committee should advise the members of the organizational skills that will be required to prepare the co-owners to assume control of the association. If there are problems with the construction or conversion of the condominium, the attorney for the advisory committee can assist advisory committee members in getting these problems resolved. If there are financial issues that perplex the co-owners, these can also be discussed by the advisory committee's attorney with the developer and his counsel.

How to pay the advisory committee's attorney is often a source of conflict and acrimony in the initial stages of condominium development. Generally the developer, as the controlling director of the condominium association, will not wish to fund the retention of counsel by his co-owners. The developer may fear that if co-owners "organize," they may disrupt the development and sale of the condominium units. He may fear that getting them legal representation may result in litigation being brought against him. The developer may be simply insensitive to the need of the association to have independent representation. In any event, in most instances in which I have had experience, the developer will not appropriate funds out of the association's budget for the retention of legal counsel for the co-owners.

What, then, has to ensue is that an organizational person must organize the co-owners and seek sufficient contributions from them to retain counsel. This should only be done after the advisory committee, or representatives of the co-owners, requests that the developer advance the funds from the condominium association. A developer should be willing to appropriate association funds to retain counsel, since his attorney, who has represented him in the development of the condominium and may also be representing the first board of directors, cannot and should not get into a potential conflict of interest situation by representing the co-owners.

The attorney chosen by the advisory committee should prepare the co-owners to take control. One of his major tasks will be to explain to the co-owners what the turnover of the association really means. Often, the co-owners are concerned that, if they accept control of the association, the developer will be relieved of his legal responsibilities incident to the commitments he has made in the condominium documents and purchase agreements. That is generally not the case, since the change in control of the condominium association is merely a change in the composition of the directors, with the result that the co-owners, for the first time, are empowered to run the affairs of the association, collect money, hire counsel and do other things that are necessary to operate the business of the condominium project.

If the association does not retain counsel on behalf of the co-owners before turnover, that should be one of the first things that the newly elected board undertakes. As previously discussed, the board should conduct a physical audit, a legal audit, a financial audit and an operational audit, under the general direction of the association's attorney, to insure that the condominium is in a proper state of affairs.

PICKING THE RIGHT ATTORNEY

How can the board of directors be sure that it picks the right attorney, and what factors should the board consider when doing so? The question cannot be answered without a clear understanding of the association attorney's post-turnover role, and can perhaps best be answered by citing examples of mistakes that, too frequently, the board of directors will make in doing so.

It should be clear to the reader that the attorney, particularly in the initial stages of condominium association operation, may be the board's most important consultant, because the attorney will assist the association to evaluate and address both the legal and financial problems that it is likely to find. It's hard, sometimes, to convince recent purchasers that they need a lawyer, particularly before turnover. Nevertheless, the association's attorney should be given the responsibility to collect overdue assessments, enforce restrictions, communicate with the developer to resolve problems with construction or conversion and with the condominium documents and assist the board to understand and discharge its fiduciary and legal responsibilities.

Many times, the developer has selected a management company that the new board wishes to continue using. Frequently, and logically, the directors ask the management company to recommend an attorney to represent the association.

Although management companies presumably are in a position to assess attorneys, one must remember that management companies are not immune from conflicts of interest, which may influence their recommendations as to attorneys and other contractors. Allow me to use fictitious characters to illustrate some finer points.

Seymour Schlemiel has a favored attorney he recommends to the boards of directors of projects he represents. Seymour likes C.C. Cheap, since C.C. Cheap and Seymour have worked together on a number of projects and C.C. Cheap is "cheap."

Seymour likes C.C. Cheap because he contributes to Seymour's strategy to find the cheapest people possible for the association, which enables Seymour to keep assessments low and makes Seymour a "hero" to its members. Moreover, C.C. Cheap does personal work for Seymour and they share investments and an office building owned by Seymour. In a word, they are very "thick." Consequently, Seymour has recommended C.C. Cheap to at least 150 condominium associations. As a result, it has become dangerous and financially risky for either C.C. Cheap or Seymour to criticize or "blow the whistle" on one another. Of course, none of these facts are disclosed to the condominium association by either Seymour or C.C. Cheap.

Seymour recommends C.C. Cheap to the board of directors of "Blue Collar Condo." C.C. Cheap has apparent credibility since, being cheap and so often recommended by Seymour, C.C. Cheap represents many condo associations. Seymour knows that C.C. Cheap is likely to appeal to the Blue Collar board because C.C. is "low-key" and has hired a young associate from the Louisiana bayou (cheaply, of course) who, with his Southern drawl and "boy next door" demeanor, will appeal to a Blue Collar board that is uptight about lawyers in the first place.

Of course, the directors of Blue Collar don't understand that, the costs of business being what they are, C.C. Cheap is not as cheap as he represents. His hourly rates may be deceptively low; that is, he may charge 1/4 hour of his time for each phone call, regardless of length. His services may reflect his lack of competence and inattention to client needs. As they say, "you get what you pay for."

Since the board of directors is serving without compensation and, presumably, without appreciation from the members, it should realize (although it frequently does not) that it should hire the best attorney available to help it run the affairs of the association. The best attorney available may not be the cheapest or, for that matter, the most expensive. The best attorney available is the one who has the relevant experience and whose reputation in the legal community as a condominium expert will enhance his ability to get results from judges and adversaries. He should have the office staff and equipment necessary to efficiently represent the association and a reputation for fair, honest and reasonably aggressive representation of condominium associations. Finally, the best attorney will maintain his independence from financial or personal relationships with other people or entities serving the condominium project, thereby avoiding even the appearance of a conflict of interest.

In most jurisdictions, the association will have a choice of attorneys with at least 15 to 20 years of experience in condominium law. Again, the board should not fall into the trap of hiring the cheapest lawyer, or of blindly hiring a lawyer the management firm recommends, or of hiring a board member's friend.

The association should review the attorney thoroughly, ask for references and ask the proper questions of the attorney in order to evaluate his or her availability, independence and abilities. What law school did the attorney attend? How many people does he have on his support staff? How many associations does he represent and is he able to represent all of these associations adequately? How does he calculate his hourly rate? What is the minimum charge for a phone call or a consultation? Does he bill in increments of a quarter hour, a tenth of an hour or by some other method? Does he have any flat rate fees for collection or bylaw enforcement procedures? What is his record of success in construction defect cases, assuming that this is one of the association's concerns? Is he recognized in the community as a condominium law expert? Do developers and lawyers fear him as a seasoned and competent proponent of the association's concerns, or is he a laid-back guy who will not stand up for the rights of the association? Will he stand independent of the management firm and raise concerns about abuses or problems that he may see from a management standpoint? Does he attend or conduct seminars, teach classes, write columns and otherwise keep abreast of the evolving changes in community association law? Is he available when you need him, by phone or otherwise, and can you get along with him? Is he or she free of any proprietary interest in the association or project?

After considering these factors, the board may well determine that C.C. Cheap is not their man. The board should, of course, interview him, and it should dig into his background. The board should keep in mind that what may appear to some directors to be a relatively mundane legal procedure may, as a matter of proper legal practice, be more complex. For instance, managing agents and directors frequently question the cost to place and record a lien on a unit for unpaid assessments and, subsequently, start collection procedures. Unless the attorney has a great deal of experience with the prosecution of collection matters, he will not know the intricacies and subtleties of federal and state debtor protection laws, far less the alternatives which are available under the condominium documents and statutes. Moreover, the association attorney's collection expertise may be critical in determining whether the association is able to recoup its attorney fees and costs.

Generally, the attorney will charge an hourly rate based upon his experience, expertise and market conditions. An association that hires a lawyer based upon cost alone will not necessarily find a good one who will pursue its interests. The association actually may end up paying more if it hires a lawyer who is incompetent, inefficient or unable to effectively serve his clients in relevant legal practice areas. Moreover, once the association is "locked in," the cheap lawyer may raise his rates or charge the same rate for all the lawyers in his firm who possess less experience or expertise!

I do not mean to suggest that Seymour Schlemiel, our property manager, cannot be of assistance to the board of directors in its search for the best attorney. In fact, for every Seymour, there is a Joe Juggernaut, who, as a relatively independent property manager, will advise the board that it should hire the best attorney it can afford, considering that many of the costs incurred by the association can be recouped from the defaulting co-owner, and that competent legal advice may enable the association to avoid the far greater expense of litigation. Will the association be able to retain the attorney on a monthly retainer basis for fixed services, or should it be on an "as needed" basis only? Finally, Joe will recommend that he examine the fee agreement between the attorney and the association.

In summary, the association should be less mindful of the hourly rate and more concerned about the caliber and value of representation that it will receive. There is no reason to accept less than proper representation for the association, to compromise the interests of the co-owners or to needlessly subject the co-owners and directors to potential liability. Remember the old Cantonese expression: "He who charges least knows best what he is worth." Nor should there be any improper relationship between the management company and attorney; both should be independent and serve as a "check and balance" for condominium administration. A good question to ask your attorney is whether he would be in a position to sue your management company, if necessary. If he says no, you should seek another, and more independent, attorney!

PICKING THE RIGHT CPA AND INSURANCE AGENT

Generally, when the association picks a CPA or insurance agent, the managing agent or attorney may be a source of referral, but the board of directors should conduct an independent evaluation of the candidates. The association should avoid hiring a professional who in any way is involved with or related to the association, either as the owner of a condominium or an immediate relative of an owner. Indeed, this applies to any professional considered by the association. A CPA may be hired to audit the association's books and to assist the board to set up a financial structure at the condominium. If the association has a professional management company, the latter should work with the association's CPA to satisfy the tax laws and place the record keeping aspects of association operations on a basis consistent with sound accounting and business principles.

The insurance agent that the association hires should not be picked because he is a cousin of a board member or is our friend Seymour Schlemiel's sister-in-law. Rather, the insurance consultant should be able to provide an objective and valuable service to the board in ascertaining the nature, extent and amount of insurance necessary to safeguard the association and its directors and officers. He or she must have a keen knowledge of the insurance problems unique to condominiums, such as the scope of coverage to the units and common elements, indemnification protection for the association and the directors, and more.

The board of directors will use the advice of these service-related persons to make important decisions that are the board's responsibility. They should not be picked arbitrarily or capriciously. Each consultant should maintain a perspective of independence and, ideally, should be the "cream of the crop" in their profession.

Of course, when things go wrong, the persons who scream the loudest about the assessments being levied will be the first to jump on the board if it makes a mistake in judgment because it did not pick the best consultants or other professionals. That's human nature and is as much the case in condominiums as anywhere else. There is no reason, therefore, for a board to shortchange itself when hiring the attorneys, property managers, CPAs, insurance consultants and other professionals necessary to help the board discharge its affairs. The "penny wise, pound foolish" maxim applies, and it should be avoided at all costs.

CHAPTER 10

Skeletons in the Closet
Potential Problems for Condominium Associations

I'm reasonably confident that of all the topics in this book, this one will need an appendix sooner than the others. The intent here is to alert the reader to some of the relatively unique problems of condominium association operation that might not be considered by the novice board member.

Being a director is a thankless job that calls for the application of keen managerial skills to unique business operations. Typically, the person who accepts a position on the board expects that it will require only that he or she attend a few meetings and make a few decisions concerning the amount of assessments, the person who will be the landscape contractor and the like.

Unfortunately, condominium operation, as with most other types of business operation, is becoming increasingly complex.

For example, 20 years ago no one talked about radon gas and its potential ramifications. However, the significance of the problem of radon gas for condominiums is potentially awesome—they are ingredients that are indigenous to certain types of structures or land that may prove to be potentially hazardous to the health and safety of humans. (The reader may desire to substitute "asbestos," "mold," "uri-formaldehyde" or "soil contaminants" for radon gas.)

Is the condominium association equipped to deal with such problems? Has the association inherited a condominium project that was converted from an apartment that contained dangerous levels of uri-formaldehyde? Does the condominium sit on property that contains excessive levels of lead or mercury, or an underground oil or gasoline storage tank? What are the consequences for the association if this is the case? Does the association have any responsibility to ensure that these are not a menace? What about potential civil liability to the association under state and federal environmental laws?

Problems with the environment may be expected to remain a major source of concern in condominiums. Garbage disposal, sanitary sewer problems, water supply and, in some instances, air pollution also will be among these. The very fact that condominiums may be deemed "quasi-municipalities" by the courts will focus additional attention on the "due process" and "equal protection of the law" rights which condominium co-owners have vis-à-vis the association. It would not be shocking if the courts were to deem the operation of a condominium to be analogous to "state action," with the result that the members of the association are afforded constitutionally-guaranteed rights vis-à-vis the association and its directors.

And then there is the area of employer liability. Yes, the association may hire employees, particularly if the board of directors has opted for self-management. What happens when the manager is accused by the assistant manager, who is an Asian female with a disability, of making unwanted remarks that are sexually suggestive, or that disparage her sex, ethnicity or physical ability? Does the board of directors have a sense of its responsibility and the potential liability to the association under federal and state civil rights statutes and other applicable laws?

Discrimination can exist in a condominium hierarchy and management structure, as in any other commercial setting. Claims of the violation of one's "civil rights" in employment and living opportunities are becoming increasingly prevalent in condominiums. The board of directors normally has no appreciation of the extent of the association's potential liability or the attendant attorney fees and costs that may result if litigation is commenced. Condominium associations are not immune, moreover, from civil rights intervention by the Justice Department on behalf of condominium residents. The Federal Fair Housing Act strictly prohibits discrimination in residential housing against the "handicapped" and, with the single exception of qualified senior housing projects, discrimination based on "familial status."

The association's board, as well as its managing agent and legal counsel, should have a keen understanding of the civil rights and employment laws. Many states have undermined the concept that a person can be terminated from his or her employment without cause. Board members tend, erroneously, to disregard employment concepts, both because they are serving as volunteers and because the nonprofit corporation is not designed to make money. On the other hand, while the directors of a condominium association may be exposed to liability to the same extent as a director of a "for-profit" corporation, they may not have the same concern for insurance protection.

Another area that may pose problems for condominiums is the air space and water rights of condos and their environs. Disputes have arisen concerning the rights of upstream or downstream users in streams and navigable waters that pass through a condominium, and the rights of the condominium association to maintain exclusivity of use within portions located within the condominium boundaries. In one instance, an association was concerned because the restrictions were not specific on whether a seaplane could be docked at the condominium boat wells, which were on a lake.

Finally, one should not underestimate the security responsibilities of condominium associations. Increasingly, co-owners expect the association to maintain adequate security within the confines of the condominium premises. Guardhouses may not be enough. Additional lighting may not be enough. The budgets of associations may have to be increased to provide a heightened level of security, not only because the association members wish or expect it, but also because the courts and the events of 9/11 and Hurricane Katrina may mandate it.

In short, the sky and the crust of the earth are literally the limits when considering changes that may take place in condominium operations and the need, therefore, to revise restrictions, rules and regulations to anticipate them. Forward-thinking drafters of condominium documents must consider potential changes in technology and the environment and their potential impact upon the condominium project. Surely these are questions that should be revisited by attorneys, developers, associations, management companies and legislators.

CHAPTER 11

Words of Wisdom
Final Thoughts and "Meisner's Maxims" on Condo Living

We all have a vested interest in seeing to it that this important and pervasive type of housing is successful. Some day, you may sell your home or move from your apartment into a condominium. You may live in a condominium as your first residence. You may dream of a second home, probably a condominium, in a warm, beautiful place. You may buy a condominium as an investment or a residence for your son or daughter during the college years.

That problems in condominium living exist will not be a revelation to anyone who has lived in a condominium. In fact, the word has probably gotten out about what it's really like to live in a condo. Even *The New York Times* has discussed how the board of directors of condominium associations may spend hours debating the paint color on mail boxes or whether the management company should be able to charge time to come to meetings.

Government intervention alone is not the answer. I was an outspoken opponent when deregulation occurred in Michigan. Nevertheless, I do not believe that broad government regulation is appropriate.

Ultimately, government cannot regulate every aspect of condominium operation. Admittedly, in the past I have encouraged the close regulation of condo developers. I still believe that the regulation of condominium development could be enhanced through closer scrutiny of the condominium documents and sales documents prepared by developers and their attorneys.

Conversely, the operational structure of the condominium association, once turned over to the members, should be relatively free from government intervention. Sure, there ought to be statutes relating to how associations pursue claims against the developer or co-owners. There also ought to be guarantees of basic co-owner rights when confronted by an aggressive or abusive condo association. Generally, however, the operation of the condo board should be laissez-faire.

A PROPOSED SOLUTION

There is a future for condos. Whether that future will be marred by problems such as those discussed in this book may depend on whether steps are taken to improve their operational structure and to educate the public concerning their proper operation. I hope that the perceptions, conclusions and cynicisms expressed in this book are received, reviewed, digested, crystallized and transformed into energized and directed momentum toward better condominium governance.

What is clear is that the present structure of condominium operation by volunteer board members who have been drafted or coerced, or who are obsessed with power, must be radically changed. I hope that this book will elicit comment and stir controversy, since there needs to be a broad-based discussion of the operation of condo associations. Those involved in condo association operation should applaud such an examination. While there may be differences of opinion as to how best to improve condominium association operation, there can be little disagreement that improvement is needed.

A new structure of condominium management should be considered. Board members should be professionalized. Perhaps a professional chief executive officer (someone from the outside) should assist in the operation of the condo. Politics should be discouraged. Power politics should be eliminated.

All parties need a better understanding of the enabling documents that regulate condo associations and community associations. This is not to suggest that they must be lawyers, but it will require them to take time and make the effort. Directors must understand their role in the community association and the legal relationship between the condo association, its members, the developer, the management agent, the local municipality and any state condominium regulatory body. Notwithstanding the inherent reluctance of co-owners to do so, directors should be encouraged to spend money on important items.

State and local governments should encourage board member and management consultant education as a condition to participate in the affairs of a condo association. Hopefully, it will not be necessary for the government to legislate mandatory education of directors, management consultants and the like, although the certification and licensure of management companies would be helpful.

It also would be helpful if condominium purchasers were better informed when they became members of an association. The purchaser of a condominium must have access to accurate information that will lead to reasonable expectations. This starts with a crackdown on those developers and advertisers who "paint" an erroneous and unreal picture of condo living. The real estate broker who solicits customers for condos also must portray what the purchaser reasonably may expect from the condominium milieu. Before they buy, purchasers should be encouraged to read books such as this and to seek the advice of legal counsel.

If the volunteer association board is to be maintained, board continuity could be enhanced by requiring that the terms of directors be staggered and that competent support staff be recruited to assist the board in making decisions. Personality clashes can be avoided by an enlightened electorate that gets to know potential candidates for the board before electing them. Being on the board ought not to be either a door prize or a booby prize, nor should it be bestowed on the person solely because he or she has expressed an interest. Hopefully, apathy will wane when association members realize that their financial investment is at risk and that their unwillingness to appreciate or encourage capable candidates serves to undermine their own investment. While the elimination of Nazi-like members from the board cannot be guaranteed, when this personality type appears, the other board members should be able to stymie their attempts to exert their will to the detriment of the association. Forceful leadership is good. Autocratic rule is not!

Condos have left their mark on society! Condos also have left their mark on the people involved in them. I have frequently been told by people who live in condos that they will never do it again. I have uttered that pronouncement myself. In one of my recent classes, I was reminded by a co-owner of a condo that his priest still will not let the condominium association hold a meeting in his parish church, 10 years after he was forced to evict its unruly members from the church hall. I find that not only to be incredible, but also rather sorrowful. Perhaps it's a harbinger of the direction in which many condos have gone and will go unless necessary improvements are implemented. Hopefully, some of the ideas, thoughts and concerns that this book explores will have a therapeutic and constructive effect on those who are willing to take the time to both read and digest its contents.

MEISNER'S MAXIMS

Over the years I have developed notions concerning patterns of conduct and common scenarios which occur in dealing with condominium boards and community associations. What follows are what are affectionately and proudly entitled (tongue in cheek) "Meisner's Maxims." These postulates have not been empirically tested, but, chances are, if you ever have any experience in dealing with a condominium association or community association, you will encounter them at some time.

If the reader who develops his or her own maxims of condo operation wishes to send them to the address listed in the References section, I will be happy to consider their inclusion in a sequel to this book!

MEISNER'S MAXIM NO. 1

"A decision of a condominium governing body is not equal to the sum of the individual opinions shared by its members."

Those that are well-versed in algebra will no doubt take me to task regarding Meisner's Maxim No. 1, but I believe that it is true. Boards make decisions rather whimsically, and the group decision often is not a composite of the opinions of the individual board members. Chances are that if you polled the board on a decision that was made by the whole group, the individual opinions of board members would not add up to the decision made by the board.

What I am suggesting is that board members make compromises, change their feelings, are intimidated and, in some cases, simply don't care about issues that come before them. They may have individual opinions but go along with either the "group" or the lead of the member who usurps power and imposes his or her will on the rest of the board. This phenomenon often results in illogical and inane decisions by boards who have failed to think through the ramifications of their decisions.

MEISNER'S MAXIM NO. 2

"Behind every board member is a person(s) pulling a string."

This maxim is analogous to the notion that our politicians do not act for themselves, but are merely the servants of special interest groups. In the condominium context, the "special interest group" may be the spouse, live-in friend or mother of the board member, or perhaps his "fishing buddy" who lives across the street. Board members have friends, relatives, in-laws and business partners who live in or have a financial interest in the condominium. He or she wants to serve the needs of his "constituents" and, when his string is pulled, the board member reacts. It's reality in the dynamics of condominium operation and, presumably, many other groups.

MEISNER'S MAXIM NO. 3

"Even when it's too hot in the kitchen, certain board members won't get out."

Board membership is a thankless task which one may expect to require the substantial expenditure of time and, more often than not, to result in criticism. Although not everyone is cut out to serve on a board, there are some people who just don't realize that they are among them. They may appreciate the complexity of the job, but they really don't have the time or ability to handle it.

Regardless of whether they are doing a competent job, these directors are like fixtures whose lights may dim, but are never replaced. They go on and on, making little or no contribution, and end up being revered, believe it or not, by those naive souls in the condominium who respect longevity. After all, if you've been there long enough, you must know what you are doing!

MEISNER'S MAXIM NO. 4

"Spend as little money as possible ... at whatever potential cost"

Some directors will, no doubt, have the perception that they should be as penurious as possible, at whatever potential cost. They do not care whether the association gets proper legal advice, for they will somehow make the decisions on their own or will rely on the managing agent's "legal advice." They will not retain a landscape contractor because one of the retired persons at the condo will cut the grass. They will not fund any money for reserves since they'd rather have the money in their own bank. They will go to small claims court to save the association the money it costs to have an attorney file a lien and pursue effective legal action. Their contribution to the members of the association, they believe, is that they have done everything they can do to avoid spending money. If things get screwed up, they can always say to neighbors, "Hey, I saved you money and you didn't have to pay me for it!" (Of course, those neighbors also got what they paid for.)

MEISNER'S MAXIM NO. 5

"What has been learned will be forgotten, ignored or placed in purgatory."

The directors and officers of condo associations are not students of history. They generally do not learn from their mistakes. They ignore their past experiences and contradict themselves, sometimes merely for the sake of contradicting themselves. Often, the same people aren't around to learn from prior experiences or from those who preceded them. Often, new people coming on the board don't want to know what the previous board has done or experienced because they think that the new board should "make a fresh start." And then, of course, we have directors who are serving on the board for a second time and want to correct what they did the first time!

In short, this maxim holds that stagnation and circuity are rampant. The board revolves in circles (sometimes taking seven to 10 years to complete a revolution) and then starts again at the beginning—except that the project has depreciated without any real progress being made.

MEISNER'S MAXIM NO. 6

"If you want to win friends and influence people, don't live in a condominium ... and don't serve on its board."

There are, of course, some directors of condominiums who will do whatever is possible to satisfy everyone at the condo, which, of course, they cannot hope to do. They believe that, in the residential context, they should be as pleasant as possible to their neighbors. They won't last long at a condo because their neighbors will eat them up, either by disregarding the restrictions or imposing their will.

There are other directors who do whatever they please because they don't care what their neighbors think. They may be egotistical or narcissistic, and may recognize that serving on the board is their chance to dominate someone else. They won't be able to dominate everyone, and they may get beat up themselves, psychologically and sometimes physically.

No, the best thing for those who want to win friends and influence people is to stay out of association affairs. In fact, if you want to win friends and influence people, don't get involved in a condominium in the first place. If you buy a condo, you are going to be encouraged to serve on the board. That's the best way to lose friends.

It's like becoming president of the United States. It's different when you are up there—you look at your friends or peers (and they look at you) differently. There is a transformation from someone who is perceived as civil and rational to someone who is engulfed in the group dynamics of neighbors engaged in self-management of community affairs. You are better off buying a farm house or even living in an apartment where the only controlling person you have to deal with is the landlord!

MEISNER'S MAXIM NO. 7

"He who works best, works least."

This is a curious maxim, in that it goes against the Protestant work ethic that is the backbone of American capitalism. The truth is that in condominium associations, the board members try to do all the work and, generally, the work is not completed or done well in such condominiums. Simply put, the directors are not merely making policy decisions, but also are responsible to implement the policy decisions.

You probably have seen it if you have lived in a condominium. The directors cut the grass, paint the complex and grab you by the arm, warning you that you cannot walk your dog and allow it to defecate on the condominium common elements. No, the best directors are ones who work the least, who delegate their tasks to people who are experienced in carrying out the prerogatives and policies of the board—management companies, accountants, insurance consultants, attorneys and the like. These directors go to their board meetings and make policies, but they aren't shoveling the snow or generating unnecessary heat.

MEISNER'S MAXIM NO. 8

"Liberty and the pursuit of happiness are unconstitutional."

Lest you think for one minute that your condominium association is a democracy and that you are entitled to due process, equal protection of the laws and happiness, buy a condo and live there for a time! As soon as you receive a dunning letter from the association that threatens to cut off your utilities because you have been slow in paying your assessments, you will not be happy. As soon as you receive a letter that your dog has been observed to have pooped in too many places, or that you parked your car in the visitor parking spot, you are going to feel that you are being harassed.

Why can't you put up the American flag on your front lawn? Because the board has told you that it is an exterior modification for which you need the board's written approval, which is denied because the board doesn't like the size of the stars on your flag. (Indeed, in Michigan they had to pass an amendment to the condo act allowing a co-owner to display the American flag on the exterior of his unit.) Moreover, as they will point out to you, they have a right to enforce the condo documents, and when you bought the condominium, you agreed to adhere to the rules and regulations.

The lawyer for the condo association even points out to you that there is case law to the effect that, when you buy a condominium, you inherently give up certain liberties that you would have in other types of housing. You can't refute that proposition, but somehow you think it's not right. But it is right because that's the reality of condo living.

If you want to be happy, as the song goes, "Be Happy," but probably in some other type of residential setting. And don't forget, if you breach the condominium restrictions after a judge orders you to comply, you could "go to jail" without "passing Go."

MEISNER'S MAXIM NO. 9
"Shakespeare was right in saying 'kill the lawyers', but wait until the lawsuit is completed."

Now there is one area where all condominium co-owners

agree. They may disagree on the company that should pick up the garbage, or on whether the assessment should be increased to build an addition to the pool, or on whether it is right to allow non-residents to participate in Mah-jongg parties in the clubhouse. They all will agree that there is no useful purpose for lawyers in the condominium or, for that matter, in society as a whole, and they will do what they can to do without lawyers. However, they will generally come to that conclusion only after they have been compelled to use a lawyer, presumably in a lawsuit, after which they will, no doubt, figuratively "kill the lawyer!"

Under this maxim, it does not matter whether the lawyer has prevailed in the lawsuit. If the lawyer charges the association for his services, the maxim requires that he be terminated. The maxim requires that in a condominium, all co-owners who have had to pay assessments to the association and also, perhaps, special assessments for legal fees, must join in at the association's annual meeting in singing "let's kill the S.O.B.!"

MEISNER'S MAXIM NO. 10
"In any condo hierarchy, an individual will fall to his level of incompetence."

At the risk of offending Lawrence Peter (the founder of the "Peter Principle"), although the Peter Principle may apply to the person who is elevated to a position on a condominium association board with responsibilities that he is incapable of handling, we also have the antithesis. The person who is well-skilled in his other endeavors falls to a common level of incompetence as soon as he joins the board of directors. The typical example of this phenomenon is the prominent corporate executive or physician who abandons his training, background, experience and common sense and gets into fights with other board members, fails to support the spending of funds, when necessary, and reverts to social gathering or country club behavior—i.e., he avoids at all cost "stepping on the neighbors' toes." He, therefore, becomes an ineffectual director and meekly descends to the lowest common denominator of the board.

MEISNER'S MAXIM NO. 11
"Time shrinks to do work."

Parkinson's Law says that "work expands to fill the time available for its completion," and, consequently, directors will make work for themselves or create controversy to satisfy a need or void in their life. Unfortunately, the antithesis is also true: There is no time for doing the work of the condo when one serves on a board.

Complacency, apathy and the notion that condo living is "carefree living" permeates the attitudes of board members. Once on the board, directors determine that they don't have time to deal with the problems or do the work attendant to their office. They don't have the time to learn about fiduciary duties. They don't have the time to read or understand the condo documents. They don't have the time to develop necessary skills. In short, whatever goes on is undertaken by the person who has allowed his work to expand to fill his time. One or two people do all the work and the other board members do little, or nothing.

MEISNER'S MAXIM NO. 12
"If something can go wrong in the condominium, it will."

This maxim is, admittedly, an offshoot of Murphy's Law, adapted to condominiums. You will recall from Murphy's Law that, if something can go wrong, it will. Well, in condos if something can go wrong, it not only will, it will be worse than any place else, perhaps resulting in litigation or a special assessment.

A further corollary to this maxim is that, for years to come, neither the board of directors nor the co-owners may realize what has gone wrong. Generally, it will take the new purchaser who, having moved into the condo, is so offended by the conduct of the board of directors that he gets stirred up. If that co-owner has some business law background or is an advocate of civil rights, he may confront the board. All hell may break loose if the board is confronted by this "recalcitrant" co-owner over policies of the board of directors that have been meekly accepted by the other co-owners for many years, even though these policies have been spawned in mediocrity, illegality, or non-logic.

MEISNER'S MAXIM NO. 13

"The 'Golden Rule' is too expensive to follow in a condominium."

Most condo owners, if asked if they believe in the Golden Rule, would answer that they do. That is, that they should treat their neighbor in the same fashion as they would like to be treated.

Of course, that maxim is much too costly in a condominium. There are directors who perceive that priorities must be set regarding the condo operations, particularly concerning maintenance and repair items. The truth in a condo is that repairs will be made to some roofs, but not to others. Concessions will be made to certain co-owners, but not to others. Modifications will be allowed to some co-owners, but not to others. Assessments will be collected from some co-owners, but not from others. All of this is because, in the condominium, uniform treatment and equal treatment are not widely practiced, and it's just too expensive. Plus, it is hard to be fair.

MEISNER'S MAXIM NO. 14

"The more things change on the board of directors, the worse they get!"

An irrefutable axiom in condo operation is that when new directors come on the board, they feel they must redo and undo everything that previously has taken place. The change is generally manifested by a desire to replace the management company, the insurance agent or the lawyer (particularly, if they can find a cheaper one). The upshot is that new people are brought in who, together with these new directors, must grapple with the learning process. Policies that were set by previous boards are dismantled or forgotten. Old ideas are pushed aside.

The board tries to reinvent the wheel. In a condo operation, frequently that's exactly what happens. Many times, depending upon the caliber of the board elected, the wheel comes out square the first six months to a year and never turns smoothly again.

MEISNER'S MAXIM NO. 15

"The more affluent the condo, the cheaper the condo."

Some readers won't grasp this concept or, at least initially, be willing to accept it. Nevertheless, those of us who have had experience with condos—and with people who have attained a certain level of wealth—have come to appreciate that financial success does not guarantee that one will be more enlightened, generous or businesslike.

To the contrary, and rather remarkably so, the more affluent a condominium association, the more penurious (cheap) that association may be. Certainly, the tendency of the co-owners toward arrogance, enlarged egos and inflated perception of knowledge and intelligence also make it difficult to represent the affluent condominium. But frankly, they're always looking for a deal. They don't pay retail for anything—and sometimes they just don't pay, period!

No doubt you've run across these people in your experiences. While they seem to gravitate towards an organizational structure, they don't want to spend money on lawyers and, in fact, they're scared to death to pay lawyer's fees. Doctors are generally the most notorious, followed closely by lawyers themselves. You would think that the more affluent condos at least would be more able and willing to spend money on the essentials necessary to properly run the association. Not true! They spend little or no money, perhaps because they perceive themselves to be experts or, perhaps, because their ex-wife's divorce lawyer "ripped them off," an experience which caused them to develop a general disdain for lawyers.

Such people may be the most difficult to organize because they all have their own perceptions of how the association should operate and are looking out for their own interests. A community atmosphere is generally less prevalent in the more affluent condos because the co-owners tend to be more individualized, pre-occupied with their diverse interests and, often, downright selfish.

Of course, what's affluent is relative. Undoubtedly, it is dependent on the geographical location in which you live. To some, an affluent condominium may be any condominium where the unit price is more than $150,000. Others may think that an affluent condominium is any condominium in which the units are in the $500,000 price range. But you'll recognize what I consider to be an affluent condo when you see the composition of its co-owners. I'm not talking about middle or even upper-middle class condos. I'm talking about condos where the people are basically multi-millionaires. Watch out in that setting!

CONCLUSION

The aforementioned (at the risk of sounding legal) Meisner's Maxims are not likely to serve you as a substitute for the Ten Commandments, the Declaration of Independence or, for that matter, the state condominium enabling statutes. Rather, they are intended only as a source of reference from which the reader may draw certain conclusions regarding the reality of living in a condominium.

If these maxims evoke controversy ... wonderful! If they encourage a professional analysis of condominium living ... wonderful (except, of course, to the extent that there may be a desire to kill lawyers)! And if these maxims cause you to chuckle ... great!

EPILOGUE

My critics may say that I have been too quick to criticize condo operations and that this analysis is not as a constructive as it might have been. Perhaps I may be thought of as arrogant and/or condescending. There may be some truth in that. I would argue, however, that if one reads this book and observes the dynamics of condo operation as they really are, they will see that there is much room for improvement. And let me say, at the risk of sounding like a politician, that I have advanced a firm program for prosperity and the betterment of condominium associations.

I do not have any preconceived notions as to how this book will be received, but I hope that it will serve as a standard text for persons who want to know what it's really like to live in a condo. I hope they will read this book before they buy a condo. I hope directors read this book before they agree to serve on boards. I hope developers read this book before they undertake to develop a condo. I hope management consultants, insurance consultants, accountants and lawyers read this before they assume the responsibilities and tasks of counseling and/or representing condo associations and/or developers.

What motivated me to write this book was, in part, a need to share my personal trials and tribulations of more than 35 years with condominium and community associations. Admittedly, writing the book was therapeutic, and to that extent it has served its purpose. If the book also serves to open the eyes of condo purchasers, condo developers, condo board members, officers, management companies and service related people, it will have far exceeded my fondest hopes and expectations.

ACKNOWLEDGEMENTS

This book has been a dream of mine for many years, and I must provide recognition to a number of individuals who assisted me and/or encouraged me in the writing of this book.

Dr. Robert Bernstein, a psychologist, felt a number of years ago that it would be a good catharsis for me to write down my thoughts and sentiments regarding the management and operation of condos based upon my experience as a practicing attorney in that field for more than 35 years. With that thought in mind, I began writing the chapters and felt that the book would be a benefit to anyone who was interested in buying and/or lived in and wished to become involved in the operation and management of a condominium.

Dr. John Vriend, a counselor, educator, and a friend for more than 20 years, also encouraged me to put my thoughts in writing, and gave me the direction I needed in an effort to obtain the publication of the book. Sincerest thanks and appreciation to David Keast, a fellow attorney and associate, who helped me with the editing and review of the manuscript.

I must also give recognition to those many persons who were associated with me over the years, both professionally and personally, who encouraged me in the practice of law and in my chosen area of specialization, including my legal assistants, M. Katherine Michael and Teresa Duddles, who have been invaluable in their assistance and help in putting together my thoughts in connection with this book.

Finally, thanks to those of you who crossed my path over these 35-plus years in the condominium field. Whether or not we were on the same side or on the same wavelength, you inspired me to write this book in an effort to help those who were interested in condominium living. To all of you, I give my sincerest thanks and gratitude.

And lastly, but not at all intended to be least, thanks to those dear to me who endured having to listen to my condo story atrocities for many years.

rm

ABOUT THE AUTHOR

Robert M. Meisner is a practicing attorney and licensed real estate broker who is a graduate of the University of Michigan and the University of Michigan Law School. Meisner has been an attorney in Michigan since 1969 and is a member of the Phi Beta Kappa Honor Society. He has been an instructor in condominium and community association law at Cooley Law School and Michigan State University/DCL Law School in Michigan, and has taught his condominium and community association courses offered to directors and officers, managers, and developers of community association through various universities and colleges throughout Michigan.

Meisner has also lectured widely through the Community Association Institute on a national level, the Institute of Continuing

Legal Education and United Condominium Owners of Michigan in Michigan, and has been a widely published columnist with the Observer & Eccentric newspapers for more than 25 years. Meisner was a co-draftsperson of the 1978 Condominium Act in Michigan, and has concentrated his law practice in the area of community association and condo law as well as commercial litigation. He practices law in Bingham Farms, Michigan.

INDEX

REFERENCES

1. Meisner & Associates, P.C.: www.meisner-law.com;

2. American Bar Association, public resources page:
www.abanet.org/public.html

3. Community Associations Institute: www.caionline.org

4. United Condominium Owners of Michigan:
www.ucomonline.org

5. Seven Pack©: A series of form procedures, rules and agreements custom drafted by Meisner & Associates, P.C. law firm
designed to follow with and complement the condominium

documents of a particular project and to facilitate its operations, and which include a Delinquent Assessment Collection Policy, a Bylaw (and Rules) Enforcement Policy, a Fine Procedure, Rules and Regulations Regarding Satellite Dishes and Antennas, two (2) Agreements to Modify Common Elements for Standard Modifications and for Persons With Disabilities, a form Lease Agreement, and a form Service Contract.

6. "Condominium Operation: Getting Started and Staying on the Right Track," 2nd Edition (2002) by Robert M. Meisner

For copies of the above booklet or to contact the author:

Robert M. Meisner
Founding Member
Meisner & Associates, P.C.
30200 Telegraph Road
Suite 467
Bingham Farms, MI 48025-4506

e-mail: bmeisner@meisner-associates.com
Web: www.meisner-law.com
(248) 644-4433
(800) 470-4433